MY CAT
SPIT MCGEE

Also by Wille Morris
and available in Beeler Large Print

MY DOG SKIP

MY CAT
SPIT McGEE

WILLIE MORRIS

BEELER LARGE PRINT
Hampton Falls, New Hampshire, 1999

Library of Congress Cataloging-in-Publication Data
Morris, Willie.
  My cat Spit McGee / Wille Morris
  p. cm.(large print)
  ISBN 1-57490-247-4 (alk. paper)
  1. Morris, Willie. 2. Authors, American-20th century Biography.
3. Cat owners—Mississippi—Biography. 4. Cats—Mississippi—
Anecdotes. 5. Large type books. I. Title.
PS3563.O8745 Z47 1999b
813'.54-dc21
[B]   99-054228

Published in Large Print by arrangement with
Random House, Inc.

BEELER LARGE PRINT
is published by
Thomas T. Beeler, *Publisher*
Post Office Box 659
Hampton Falls, New Hampshire 03844

Typeset in 16 point Adobe Garamond type
Printed on acid-free paper and bound by
Sheridan Books in Chelsea, Michigan

To my friend Bailey Browne, eleven years old and a girl, very pretty and a little shy, who personally asked me to write a book about my having hated cats forever and then grown to care for them, especially Spit Mcgee.

And to every person who ever loved a cat.

Contents

MY CAT
SPIT McGEE

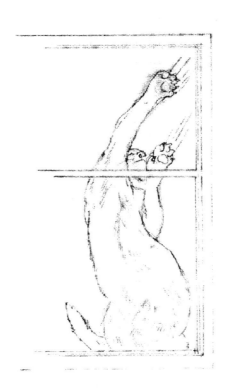

CHAPTER 1

ALWAYS A DOG MAN

As I write these opening words, I pause to gaze out the windows of my upstairs workroom onto the broad lawn and to the creek beyond, which we call Purple Crane. I sight Spit McGee there, more likely than not communing with his companion, the big noisy bullfrog who has resided in these waters ever since we moved into this house five years ago.

Spit's clean white fur glistens in the autumn sun. In the brightest of sunshine he can be almost invisible in his whiteness, but I know his silhouette. He strides closer to the creek. He has a jaunty walk for a large cat; if human he would be either a catcher or a third baseman. Sometimes he senses when I am looking down at him, because there is something like that between us, and he will turn and stare up at my window in recognition, but on this day he is concentrating on the bullfrog.

He is eight years old now, contented, I believe, and in

1

good health. In all those years he has been with me. It was I, in fact, who actually delivered him at birth, and I have saved his life four times. In the ancient Oriental dictum, if you save a fellow creature's life just once, it is your responsibility to watch over him forever.

My wife says Spit is my factotum. I will admit to serving as his valet, butler, and menial, daily and in perpetuity, and in recompense I think he consents to being my constant and abiding comrade. When we first came together, he and I had monumental arguments, disagreements, "spats" if you want to call them that. We were different. To this day we have these intermittent contretemps, but they seem part of a larger whole now. We know our foibles and try to forgive each other, for neither of us is perfect. Why on earth, out of all the countless billions of cats in the world, am I ineluctably drawn to this one? There are times, I confess, I feel an odd writer's inkling that Spit McGee is the reincarnation of my dog Skip, the beloved companion of my long-ago boyhood, whom I once wrote a book about, and about whom a movie was made; that Spit had been dispatched in the spirit of Old Skip by the Almighty to make sure I am doing okay.

But that is a very long story, and I must first digress to a most candid and pristine account of what I for the longest time thought about cats.

I had always been a dog man, as was just about everyone else I ever knew. When I was growing up we did not pay much attention to cats, and we certainly did not like them. In fact, I could not stand them.

Dogs were essential to our very existence. They were distinctive presences in the small Mississippi town where I was raised. We knew them all and called them by name. I

2

got to know all about dogs—their various moods, how they acted when they were hungry or sick, what they were trying to tell you when they made strange, human noises in their throats. My father had big bird dogs when I was very little—named Tony, Sam, and Jimbo—and my most precious moments were when they licked me on the nose, ears, and face. So when Skip came to me in the third grade, I was ready for him.

What is the mysterious chemistry that links a human being and a dog? I only know that the friendship between Skip and me, and later a black Labrador named Pete and me, was God-given, and solidified by shared experience and fidelity and a fragility of the heart. (How could there be such a compact with *cats*?) "It is easy to forget that in the main we die only seven times more slowly than our dogs," Jim Harrison, one of my favorite authors, has written. "The simplicity of this law of proportion came to me early in life, growing up as I did so remotely that dogs were my closest childhood friends." My enduring memories of Old Skip reside in my deepest being. Those readers of *My Dog Skip* may recall that I was an only child and he was an only dog, and that he was less my dog than my brother.

Boys and dogs have been allies since caveman days. We were inseparable. Older people in the town still talk about him. He could drive a car with a little help. He could play football and climb trees. He held the world record for fox terriers in the 100-yard dash. He could read my mind and had an inexplicable divination of where I might be at any given moment: the same attributions that my unlikely future Spit McGee would likewise have. We even fell in love with the same girl. He was such a part of the town that photographs of him were featured in the school yearbook. He could get into anywhere on his own if the

3

whim was upon him—my schoolroom when class was in session, picture shows, baseball games, funerals. We were together at birthdays, Christmases, and New Year's Eves. We admired the same friends and suffered the same fools. And when he died at age thirteen while I was far away in college, my parents buried him in my old baseball jacket under the elm tree in our backyard. Years later my mother donated his tombstone to the local historical museum in Yazoo City, and if any of the readers of this book wish to see it, it is to this day on honored display.

I did not have another dog for many years, until I was married and had a small son. We got him a little fox terrier who was run over and later an eccentric black Lab named Ichabod H. Crane, who met the same fate. We grieved over their demises. And then Pete came along. If Skip was the dog of my boyhood, then Pete was the one of my maturity. He was in every way as special as Skip, but he was different, although the two of them had many of the same traits: affection, loyalty, imagination, and intelligence being most notable among them.

After years in the magazine business in New York City, I moved out to a village by the sea on eastern Long Island called Bridgehampton. I was divorced and lonesome. My best moments were when my son David Rae, who was then twelve years old and living in the city, took the train from Penn Station to see me on weekends. Years later David Rae said he was the only kid in history to have a sibling rivalry with a dog.

Pete and I sought each other out, two vagabond bachelor hearts. Just as with Skip, I was drawn to him from the moment I saw him—a splendidly handsome black Labrador retriever, perhaps three years old, with brown eyes, floppy ears, and a shining ebony coat, who spent most of his time with the boys in the service station.

4

As with Skip those years and years ago, he was a ubiquitous presence in the town. I once even saw him driving around with Truman Capote. As the town's semiofficial mayor, known to all as "Your Honor," Pete patrolled its streets and its schools and its beaches and its graveyards and its whole backyard world of gardens and orchards and barns. At night he slept in bars or in pickup trucks.

He belonged to no man. Yet I perceived he was beginning to look me over. Whenever I drove into the station for gas, he would leap into my car. He relished driving around as much as Skip had. As we rode by the lush fields and sand dunes of the great Eastern littoral, he would sit there quietly, looking as if he were reflecting on me. Soon he started visiting me at my house, each visit longer than the one before.

One afternoon, however, he did not leave. "Go back, Pete," I said. "They expect you." He refused to go. If dogs carried traveling kits, he might have unpacked his razor, shaving cream, and deodorant then and there. It was a moment of rare consequence.

When, a couple of years later, I decided to leave the village on Long Island and return to my native Mississippi, to live and die in Dixie, I felt guilty about taking Pete, a Yankee dog if ever there was one, from his home soil. But tell me: Had I a choice? The car was loaded and I was ready to depart, for I had made my own aching farewells. Pete ruminated for the briefest instant, one transitory moment of profound Labrador reflection, then jumped inside. Did *he* have a choice?

He adjusted to the South, Pete did, although Oxford, Mississippi, was removed from Long Island in much more than mere distance. He took to the beauty and serenity of the Ole Miss campus, where I was the writer in residence.

5

All the students knew him from our daily walks. In the summer, he had his own watering spot, a place in the woods where he sat twice a day in the stifling humidity for a long time. I thought I discerned a hint of "y'all" in the way he barked, and he even liked collard greens, which even Skip himself, disparate as he was in his culinary habitudes and a down-home dog if ever there was one, never did.

Pete eavesdropped on my telephone conversations, just as the gifted cat Spit McGee someday would. If we had not seen my son in several months, and I said, "David Rae is coming tomorrow," Pete would rise and stretch and be ready to leave for the airport. As with Skip, we had a private language often not words so much as gestures, expressions, intuitions. We shared ancient affinities. How would I have ever known then that against all expectations I would someday have a similar relationship with a cat? Surely certain things are not possible.

In our countless travels, Pete and I were trapped, snow-bound, in a small town far away, chased by copperheads in the wooded hills behind William Faulkner's house, watched Ole Miss baseball games from the left-field bleachers. Once Shelby Foote gave us a tour of the catastrophic Civil War battlefield of Shiloh, where at one point Foote, an incorrigible fellow dog man, said, "Look at that! Pete's wading in the Bloody Pond."

Shortly after we came South, Pete ran away. More accurately, he got lost. This terrible experience reminded me in horrific aspect of the time Old Skip in my boyhood days did not return home. As with Skip's calamity, I drove everywhere looking for Pete. At night I left my back door open, listening sleeplessly to each rustle and sound. I contacted the mayor, the dog warden, and the constabulatory. I telephoned the governor. Was Pete disoriented in the impenetrable Mississippi woods? Lying dead in a ditch? Kidnapped? On the fourth day, stricken and hopeless, I sat in my house with a friend who comprehended my broken heart. She and I consumed a bottle of scotch.

Suddenly, from the crest of the hill beyond the windows, something flickered briefly in the corner of my eye. I went outside and peered through the mist. Pete was faltering down the hill. Then he saw me. As in a vintage Hollywood film, we walked slowly toward each other, old as time. He was wet, filthy, and bleeding. I embraced him there, in the middle of the road.

Pete was thirteen years old, the same age as Skip, when he died. He had grown slow and feeble. I had been taking him to the vet two or three times a week. From his suffering I knew he was fading from me. I found him one morning gasping for breath. His eyes were heavy with pain. I lay on the floor next to him. I held him in my arms and told him I loved him. He looked at me and weakly wagged his tail. Then he licked my face. After a time he stood and limped out the door. He lay down near the house. I sat with him there for a while, then left for a moment. When I came back he was dead.

Our friends made him a small oak coffin. Late that afternoon, in a dark and gloom-filled rain, we buried him on a placid old hill in the town cemetery, only a short distance from William Faulkner's grave, for the mayor had given us dispensation to do so. A few people he had cared for gathered there. One of them read from the Episcopal *Book of Common Prayer:*

> They shall hunger no more, neither thirst any more; neither shall the sun light on them, nor any heat.
> For the lamb which is in the midst of the throne shall

feed them, and shall lead them into living fountains of water: and God shall wipe away all tears from their eyes.

We put up a handmade tombstone for him: *Pete— 1971-1984. We loved you.* Years later a little boy who had known about Pete and walked by his grave every day in a shortcut to his school reported to me that someone had stolen Pete's tombstone. Never mind. As with Skip, he is there for me in the sunlight and grass and shadows, in the echoes and remembrances and passing years. I was so sorrowful I promised myself never to have another dog. "Will you get another?" friends and acquaintances always asked. "No," I would reply. "I'll get another wife first."

I wish Skip and Pete had known each other. Someday if I make it to heaven I plan to go looking first for my mother and father, and my grandmother and grandfather, and Skip and Pete. I speculate now: How would my cat, Spit McGee, have gotten along with Skip and Pete? And in the very elemental asking I believe I know: they would have been an honorable triumvirate.

CHAPTER 2

HOW I HATED CATS!

I WAS ALWAYS NOT ONLY A CAT MISANTHROPE, I TOOK pride in being one. Did I consider liking cats *unmanly?* Cat lovers, I would later read somewhere, are called "ailurophiles," and those who hate cats, "ailurophobes." Allow me to introduce myself here as one of North America's top-ranking ailurophobes of that period.

Neither Skip nor Pete ever had anything much to do with cats. Not, perhaps, because they loathed cats, to which I myself readily admit, but because they were not the least bit interested in cats. The solitary exception was a little sick stray kitten who took up with Skip for a few days, then died. Skip felt sorry for her, so I guess I did too.

No, ours was a *dog* culture in my town. There were always anxious, marginal individuals with cats hanging around—in shanties on the Yazoo River, in derelict dwellings falling in on themselves which responsible citizens had long before abandoned, so that we associated cats with crazy people. Both the people and the cats, in addition, *smelled* bad. I remember one demented old

9

woman who wandered around town in a filthy black dress festooned with cockleburs and insinuated herself by entering people's garages uninvited and cooking bacon; wherever she went she was followed by seven or eight slinking cats. Some even said she boiled cats and ate them for supper. Another familiar personage, a one-eyed man with a harelip and two thumbs on his right hand, giving him six fingers on that one hand, with enough dirt under his fingernails to cultivate a good row of corn, lived in an abandoned barn on the outskirts of town with more than thirty cats. The weekly newspaper reported that the barn was a health hazard, and after that the county dispatched its spray truck twice a month and fumigated this slovenly domicile.

My friends and their families buttressed my profound disaffection for all cats, which we universally considered dumb, vain, and coldhearted, not to mention remote, calculating, and sinister. This was of our inheritance, in fact. I was, in truth, actually afraid of cats, and this grew more physically acute as I got older. Not for one moment did I want these creatures lurking around me. All my life I had had fiendish nightmares of cats leaping onto my face and gouging out my eyes with their rapierlike claws.

We knew of men who went out in pickup trucks along the back roads and shot stray cats with .22 rifles for target practice. It was commonly known that a pair of older high school boys, the meanest boys in town, went around the countryside torturing stray cats—tying powerful firecrackers to their tails and igniting them, dousing them with gasoline and burning them alive, tying them up and dismembering them with sharpened knives. They boasted of these exploits. This back-country along the swamps and the river swarmed with loner cats living on the cusp of civilization and wildness. Many years later, when I was a student in Europe and visited the ruins of the Forum and the Coliseum in Rome, I was horrified by the dozens of feral cats who lived in grim, shadowy interstices, all bunched together and screeching and gyrating, and they reminded me in no small measure of the homeless cats of the Yazoo boondocks.

Such memories of cats abounded for me. When I was little I stayed with my grandparents and two eccentric great-aunts in the capital city of Jackson every summer. My great-aunt Maggie Harper was eighty years old and a spinster, since she grew up after the Civil War and in Mississippi there were no men to marry then. Barefoot and wearing a sailor's cap, I accompanied her on her ceaseless perambulations around the city. She had a hybrid spotted cat who followed us everywhere, a cross-eyed yellow cat I disliked so much that, although I have always taken no inconsiderable pride in my recollection for detail, I do not even remember the beast's name. Aunt Maggie had a nomadic bladder, and would pause at every fourth or fifth dwelling to "borrow" the bathroom and then to gossip with her female contemporaries, who sat on decaying verandas shrouded in crepe myrtle, surrounded by their murky, inhospitable cats, who would have nothing at all to do with Aunt Maggie's cat. Sometimes when I started a stroll around the city all by myself, her cat would try to follow me, and I would hide behind trees, garages, and garbage cans to liberate myself from him. Or was it a *her?*

My litany of feline phobias is far from complete. When we were eighteen or so, our semiprofessional baseball team from the town reached the national championship tournament in Wichita, Kansas. When we were finally defeated, the men who had driven the seven or eight cars from home somehow forgot about two other boys and me

11

and started driving the long distance south, leaving the three of us abandoned and with little more than five dollars among us. We went out to the railroad yards and hopped a freight train heading in the right direction. It was the darkest nighttime and we were in an empty car. Suddenly we saw four stray cats at the opposite end of the boxcar. In the darkness they were staring at us with wicked fluorescent eyes, which glowed from the shadows like hellish, fiery orbs. Then they began hissing like snakes. You can imagine the sight of three big boys, all dog people, cowering in terror in a corner. I carried that sorry memory with me for a long time; it became part of my cat nightmares. Lucky for us those cats jumped off the train in Memphis.

When I was a student in Oxford, England, I lived in a spooky college, a medieval fortress, really, that had been built in A.D. 1386. The most lugubrious spot in this establishment was its cloisters, crowded with the mossy gray crypts of the dead of the interminable centuries. In the center of this forbidding venue, under an ancient oak with skeleton-like limbs, lived an enormous turtle rumored to be three hundred years old. This monster loitered there all day and all night. What could a three-hundred-year-old turtle do but loiter? But the most dreadful aspect of all this was an immense black cat with teeth like venomous fangs who was the turtle's constant companion, sometimes even sleeping on the turtle's gargantuan shell; the cat was reputed to be the turtle's bodyguard. One late afternoon of ephemeral mists and rain with the venerable chimes ringing everywhere, I went in there to take a photograph of the turtle. As I was doing so, the black cat with a hideous screech leapt out at me from behind the oak tree. He jumped onto the leg of my trousers, his claws raking my skin. I let out a wail that

12

could have been heard to the Pas de Calais. I threw the camera at him, which conked him on the head. He squawked and retreated, and so too did I. Later I enlisted a friend from Tennessee who one day would be our ambassador to the kingdom of Jordan to help me retrieve my camera. Armed with a shovel and a hammer purloined from the college carpenter, we entered the cloisters on the stealthiest tiptoes. We found the camera and got out of there fast.

Cats! In New York I had girlfriends who doted on their cats. At least one flourishing romance was terminated because I could not get along with the young woman's cats. Their names were King Tut, the Count of Monte Cristo, and Rasputin, and I ended that connection because they were always glowering at me like the cats on the freight train from Wichita. I could not even abide the Algonquin cat, princeling of the hotel by that name, and when people made a great ceremonial fuss over him in the lounge or the restaurant, I could not begin to comprehend it.

Then there was the matter of a cat I called the River Cat. I was living in a cypress cabin on the green and serpentine Bogue Chitto River in remotest Mississippi. The cabin was owned by a friend who was away for several weeks, and he allowed me to use it as I was finishing a book with the understanding that I would feed his cat every day. This cat was furry black, not unlike the big cat in the college cloisters in England, and he had ebony eyes, and he did not like me very much. He would go off hunting down the river and would be gone for several days at a time; no doubt he dined on rats, lizards, snakes, and bugs. Whenever he returned, he took it upon himself to scare the senses out of me. It was lonely out there in that cabin, I can tell you, which was a little eerie in its own right, with unnatural echoes that sounded like Choctaw

13

drums rising from the farthest nocturnal horizons. I had set up work in a room in back with a table set against the windows. One ponderous twilight I was sitting there when with no warning whatsoever a hairy creature leapt onto the sill of the windows in front of me and began screeching and scratching hysterically at the outside glass as he stared menacingly at me with a gaze as mad and homicidal as any of Charles Manson's. Of course I fell out of my chair and lay sprawled for long moments on the floor. I never knew when these assaults would occur. Sometimes there would be long intervals in between, sometimes they would come upon me two or three times a week, and that book was a hard one to finish. I did not know what to make of these maddening incursions and could only conclude that cats more or less as an act of nature had it badly in for me.

Over time I grew to study certain fellow writers and *their* attitudes toward cats. I could never understand, for instance, why Hemingway, a man I admired greatly, liked cats, while his principal competitor, Faulkner, distrusted them as much as anyone. As antidote to Hemingway, I made a point to read the writer and cat expert Doris Lessing and was interested to discover that she always found cats stoic, helpless, and pitiful, objects of pathos. Then I was gratified to have William Styron, a black Lab and golden retriever man, inform me he was so disdainful of cats that whenever his daughter left her cats in his house in Connecticut to be fed when she was traveling, Styron would aridly put the food in their platter, then have nothing to do with them the rest of the day, sometimes to the point of hiding behind the furniture to avoid them. The image of the author of *The Confessions of Nat Turner* and *Sophie's Choice* hiding from cats behind a chifforobe in his very own house was uplifting for me.

14

When I was living on Long Island, however, my comrade James Jones, whom many deemed macho, cut holes in the doors of his farmhouse so his cats could go where they pleased. These were cats brought over from Paris, and he spoke to them in pidgin French, which reminded me of having once seen Humphrey Bogart dubbed in Italian. He had a cat who would sit on his shoulder while he was typing away in the attic, and this gave me second thoughts about Jones.

In similar context, I was spending some time in Virginia with the writer Edwin M. Yoder, Jr., whom I had known for more than thirty years and who had always seemed level-headed enough to me. Ed had a Siamese cat he considered to be directly descended from the royal cats in the nineteenth century court of King Mongkut of Siam. As with James Jones's stuck-up Parisian cat, this one would vault onto Yoder's shoulder and then drape himself, in the manner of a fox fur, around his neck. I thought this degrading. This cat's name was Pharaoh, and he communicated with Yoder in low, emphatic, guttural syllables—just sat there in front of his patron and *talked*. I was actually witness one evening to the owner's putting a slice of cantaloupe on the creature's dish, which he forthwith devoured, then turned to us and, I swear to God, said "*Yum! Yum! Yum! Yum!*" Yoder replied, "*Yum! Yum! Yum! Yum!*" right back, then the two of them began conversing in deep, throaty syllables reminiscent of the dialogue in the old B movie *Invasion of the Cat Monsters,* emphasizing these exchanges by histrionic movements of both their heads. Now, if you see a Pulitzer prize-winning editorialist whom you have known for Lord knows how long standing nostril to nostril with a garrulous cat and talking in the cat's language, that cannot help but give you pause about the man, and for that matter the cat. Also, the

15

arcane vocabularies this human and this cat exchanged before my eyes seemed arrogantly overspecialized, like those Eskimo dialects said to have about sixty-four words for snow. Since Yoder had fed the cat but not me, later that night when the house was quiet I invaded the refrigerator in the dark, but Mrs. Yoder was out of town and the refrigerator was empty—not even one solitary egg was in there. On a counter I detected a can of tuna fish. I opened it and ate a spoonful; it was so nauseous I spewed it out on the floor. When I looked at the can again, I noticed it said "Friskies Tuna Fish." I did not say "*Yum! Yum! Yum! Yum!*" I did not even bother to clean up the mess. Instead I left that house at the break of dawn and did not communicate with my host for six months.

Finally, I must confess in my unexpurgated truthfulness that cats once almost came between my son, David Rae Morris, and myself. Pete had recently died, and David Rae and his companion, Susanne, arrived from Minnesota to spend several days with me in Mississippi. They had two cats with them. David Rae had always been a dog man like his father. What had gone wrong? He had attached himself to a cat person, that's what. How could he so betray his own lineage? Had he no respect for the memory of Skip and Pete? We argued about this. These cats had the run of the house. Their litter box was even in my bathroom. They pampered those cats as if they were lineal scions of the House of Saxe-Coburg-Gotha. One morning I woke up in my bed to find one of the cats sound asleep *on my face*! That night when my visitors were out on the town I was sitting in the front room with a companion named Big Red, a former Ole Miss basketball player who now raised hunting dogs. "Good God!" Big Red suddenly sat up and declared, spilling his beer all over his trousers. "Do you know I just saw a damned *cat*?"

16

CHAPTER 3

FALLING IN LOVE—AND A DIRE CONFESSIONAL

THE PASSING OF PETE AND THEN THE SQUABBLE WITH
David Rae over his cats enveloped one of the lowest points
in my life, a nadir that almost every writer I have ever
known has experienced at one time or another. Or for that
matter, I guess most everybody. It was 1989. I had been
living for nearly ten years in my bungalow on the Ole
Miss campus, next door to a similar one where William
Faulkner used to come every Sunday night years before to
visit a professor friend and smoke his pipe in silence and
watch a weekly television show called *Car 54, Where Are
You?* My writing was not going well. My bank account
was precarious—I could not even afford a decent present
for Pete on the final birthday of his life—and I was
suffering from a tenacious angst and melancholia such as I
had not known since twenty years before, when I
transplanted from New York City to eastern Long Island
and Pete had yet to move in with me. I had also developed
an evil little rash on my back. My old Dodge four-door
had come up with an incurable rattle that caused Oxford

17

citizens to tarry and stare when I drove down the street; I feared it might explode at any moment. I had been divorced since 1969 and had never remarried. I will not say that I was lost, but I was surely drifting. Christmases were especially bereft. I had a bachelor Jewish pal who ran a boondocks avant-garde coffee emporium, and during the Yuletide seasons we intruded ourselves on one humane family after another for dinners, parties, and tree decorating. We called ourselves the Wandering Jew and the Wandering Gentile.

Then something totally unanticipated happened. I felt myself falling in love! The sympathetic reader deserves a substantial explanation, particularly since this is precisely why Spit McGee himself will soon enter this tale and remain there.

I got a telephone call from her one day from Jackson, 150 miles away. She was an editor with the University Press of Mississippi and wanted me to do a book in collaboration with a prominent artist. Could she come up and discuss this with me?

She was named JoAnne. (Later in this volume she will also be referred to, for ample enough reason, as the Cat Woman.) I had known her since the late 1960s, when she was married to a friend of mine and taught the gifted students in the high school in my hometown. She had also written the prizewinning history of Yazoo County. She had entered Ole Miss at precisely the same time as James Meredith, the young black man who integrated that institution. She was ten years my junior and had two inspiriting sons. She had been divorced for several years. I had not seen her in a long time.

We met in a restaurant and discussed the book. I had forgotten her beauty and disposition and finesse, the kindly and percipient heart and sense of laughter. How many loves, pray tell me, get their start because of a *book?*

She was a Delta girl, and I a Delta boy. Somehow she could change personae, swift as April rainfalls: one day she might look like a schoolteacher, the next a beauty queen, then an unabashed doyenne of the cognoscenti. There was the moment I found myself driving with her in a Delta twilight. All around in this twinkling of humanity and happiness, marred only by the intrepid rattling of my stricken Dodge sedan, were the purlieus of my own beginnings, places Old Skip and I had known so well those years ago: the cypresses in the mossy ponds, the dwindling woods, the little hardscrabble towns of my youth, the interminable flatness in the burnt orange glow. She too cared for the lingering landscapes and memories, adored Christmases, wished for snow in Mississippi even though it never came. Her father had survived the fighting in France as an infantry captain, received a Bronze Star and two Purple Hearts, and came home to see his daughter for the first time and carried her into the backyard, and her first words to him were "Daddy, see the moon?" In the Delta she had a gift for spotting egrets perched on cows' backs on the flat dark earth, and solitary hawks in the autumnal trees. Who can explain such enigmas of belonging, especially when they come late? In her backyard, on dewy springtime nights, we listened to the supple, beguiling Mississippi mockingbirds in their eternal rhyme; who would ever kill a mockingbird?

One is so terribly fearful that he cannot love again, after all the years—well, perhaps not so much that, but are you *qualified* to do so again? The crowning moment came when her sons told me about her grandmother. She had outlived her older son, JoAnne's father, who had taken care of her, and two years before, at eighty-nine years old, was in a nursing home in a small Mississippi town to the south. She did not like it there. There was no affection in it, she said. So JoAnne went down there and rescued her, pretty much kidnapped her because the nursing home could not legally release her, brought her back to her house, read to her, cooked for her, cared for her until she died a year later in her granddaughter's arms. That was pretty much it for me.

I stipulated that the wedding itself not take place for eight months or so, until as a matter of honor, pride, and chivalry I started making money again. In the weeks before our wedding, however, a most distressing thing happened. No, distressing is much too flaccid a word: *apocalyptic.* She told me she wanted to get a kitten! Her announcement, as you can only fathom, struck me in my inmost sinews. This was when I learned that I was engaged to a Cat Woman, which was considerably more than I had even remotely bargained for.

This apprehension could only heighten when she actually began confessing to me in overweening detail her perfervid relationship over the years with cats. When she was growing up in Indianola, Mississippi, she now brazenly divulged, she had an adored pet, a black, orange, and white tabby. The cat's name was Crybaby, but they always called her Kitty. When my fiancée was seven years old, the family moved to DeRidder, Louisiana, when her father was called back into the army during the Korean War; she had acquired the cat there. The cat lived until halfway through her college years.

I listened with mounting anxiety as she told me these things. Crybaby, unlike most cats, loved to ride in a car. This cat would sleep soundly on the backseat with her on the long trips they made between Louisiana and Mississippi. The cat slept with her almost every night and always jumped on her in the morning to get her up for school. Crybaby had a litter of kittens every year. Once this cat had kittens in my fiancée's doll's tester bed! JoAnne almost always had kittens to give away around Halloween. She gave one to her best friend, and the two of them would dress their cats in doll clothes and play "house" with them during the long summer days.

That was anything but the end of it. She went further to confess she always felt naturally attuned to not only *her* cat but to *all* cats. She loved the way they slept and stretched and purred. I could hardly believe what came next. She used to practice purring herself but could not master it. (Are you believing this?) She did not understand dogs at all back then, she admitted. She was, in fact, paralyzed with fear as a young girl when a dog approached her or barked at her when she was walking or riding her bicycle around Indianola. Later, when she had a family of her own, her two boys had several dogs and she grew quite attached to them. Thank God for that! But the boys always had cats, too. In fact, the mother cat and one kitten from a previous litter had kittens at the same time, so that they had *fourteen* cats. She concluded this grisly confessional, "I like to have a cat in the house. My house just doesn't feel right without a cat."

The reader can only imagine my waning spirit. Why had this woman not had the temerity to reveal these truths to me before I proposed to her in front of one thousand outstanding citizens in the Old Senate Caucus Room in Washington, D.C.? *Fourteen* cats at one time?

I was now at a loss as to what to do. I drove around Mississippi for three days thinking things out. I really cared for this woman, and I kept remembering the charitable rescue of the grandmother. I concluded I needed some sound counsel about cats.

First I approached a friend named Ben, who had until

recently always been a dog man but now because of his wife, Dorothy, had become drawn to a cat named Bill. "I always thought cats were dumb just like you do," Ben said. "But cats are smart as hell, I can tell you." Ben had to travel a lot, he reminded me. "When I pack my bag I have to hide it so Bill won't see it. Then I have to sneak out of the house with it. When I come home, he's mad at me. Won't speak to me for a whole day, Bill won't." That was all I could get out of Ben.

During a social visit a couple of days later I decided to solicit some thoughts from a perspicacious individual on all matters, Eudora Welty, whom I had known ever since I was first introduced to her by my great-aunt Maggie at the vegetable counter in the Jitney Jungle in Jackson when I was eight years old. I was aware that Eudora was not a cat person but would perhaps have an insight or two into my unusual predicament. I met her in her old Tudor-style domicile in Jackson, where she forthwith declared that her house had always been a dog house all her life. "My mother couldn't stand the thought of a cat." She remembered, however, seeing Caroline Gordon, the writer, for the first time in Greenwich Village many years ago. "I was going to meet her. I was walking along Eighth Avenue and she was carrying around a bunch of newborn kittens with her, and she'd go up to people on the street and say in this winning way, 'You look like a cat person. Wouldn't you like a kitten?' It didn't work very well. She had a good many left. Whatever became of those kittens, I've wondered."

Beyond providing this vivid Village tableau out of the 1930s, Eudora was not of too much help to me, I am afraid, but she did suggest I set up a meeting with a friend of hers, a noted psychiatrist in town who admired and indeed doted on cats.

The last thing I desired at this point, quite frankly, was for my dog-loving associates to know I was actually consulting a licensed professional psychiatrist about cats, and I have kept this tête-à-tête secret till right now. Thomasina Blissard is an honors graduate of the University of Mississippi Medical School and then Tulane Medical School for her psychoanalytical training. I met her in the den of her house as arranged, making sure none of my fellow cat misanthropes was shadowing me en route. Dr. Blissard began by declaring that she under no circumstances ever considered herself a cat psychiatrist, that she had never in her entire career recommended cats as therapy, and that she had never treated cat haters—"unless," she added with no little trace of paradox, "you count *this* as a session." She informed me at the start that in 1957 her mother gave her a book by Paul Gallico called *Thomasina: The Cat Who Thought She Was God,* which was made into a film, and to this day she considers herself blessed to bear the same name as Gallico's fabulous cat.

These were the main points of her private counsel:

Cats are as different from one another as dogs are from one another. "This comes from one who adores cats: cats can be very selective about whom they love and are friends with. With few exceptions dogs take up with people with greater ease than cats. Hence 'man's best friend.' Dogs love every person."

Since antiquity, the doctor emphasized, cats have been associated with the mystical. Therefore, some people actually fear that cats are detecting the unconscious in themselves. Cats are more isolated and distant than dogs, she said, even at times with people they live with daily and are dependent on. "Cats aren't *owned.* Cats are highly demanding. They're wonderfully self-absorbed. I felt very fortunate when my cats accepted my touch. They either accepted it or shrugged it off."

She looked me suspiciously up and down as she continued. "Men are reluctant to admit they like cats, you know. I guess they think it's unmanly to do so. But cats are splendid hunters and very sportsmanlike. Listen, you don't have to love your fiancée's cat. Leave the cat alone and he won't bother you. If he makes overtures to you, step away but don't be unfriendly, if you can possibly withhold your bad feelings about cats."

The doctor had had two Persian cats named Omar and Abou. She thought of them as "litter-mates." "I never considered them brothers because I didn't think of them as people. That's why I was able to love them so easily and unceasingly. Omar was more aloof and wouldn't always show himself to company. Abou would always go to the person in the room who most disliked cats and make him move somewhere else. Cats, like analysts, pick up on things, share insights." She again looked challengingly at me: "I learned to reconsider the characteristics of the person who was met with disdain by Abou. Sometimes Abou uncovered features I'd missed and I found I didn't care for this person either." Omar lived to be fifteen, Abou twenty. "Their presence remains in this house as you can probably tell. It was theirs all along and always will be."

I do not know what Dr. Blissard made of me, or for that matter what her psychic and incisive cat Abou might have, and I was lucky, I suppose, that he was not there that day to sift out the flaws in my interior makeup, and hence I tried to depart with grace and dignity. "Could a dog man ever like cats?" I asked. "Of course he can," she replied, and left it at that as she gently closed the door.

The reader may have already noticed that this volume has been dedicated to young Bailey Browne because she is the one who got me to do it. At this point I would most assuredly have conferred with Bailey Browne about cats, but unfortunately she was only about three years old at the time and was not quite ready for me. The next best to her, I determined, might be her mother, Jill, another confirmed Cat Woman and future author of *The Sweet Potato Queens' Book of Love,* and because she was, after all, Bailey's mother, which existentially mattered to me. As with most people here in our region, Bailey's mother is a teller of tales, rather circuitous ones at that, and after she heard my queries about cats as we sat in a bar called Hal & Mal's she chose to respond with a true story about her cat-hating uncle-in-law. "You can take this for what it's worth," she said. Somewhat reluctantly I listened her out, in the accommodating spirit of this history of mine, and solicit the reader to do so also.

Jill Conner Browne's Aunt Moggie lived with her uncle Pete in the red-dirt hills of Attala County, Mississippi, and she visited them often as a little girl. Aunt Moggie was gaga about cats and had twenty or more of them at any given time. When she made biscuits, which in a country home like that was about three times a day back then, all the cats would line up in the kitchen—not a meow would be uttered, not a paw moved, only their heads oscillating as they watched. They would line up, biggest to smallest, with the bigger ones closest to the stove. As soon as the oven door with the biscuits inside was shut, pandemonium erupted. In unison all twenty-odd cats would stand up on their hind legs and commence an awful howling and dance all around the kitchen until Aunt Moggie gave them scraps of the biscuit dough. This occurred every time she made biscuits for as long as she lived. Cats would die and new cats be born and the tradition was passed down.

All of this was to the supreme and indigenous disgust of

Moggie's husband, Uncle Pete, an infamous curmudgeon and self-proclaimed hater of cats. He was always threatening to drown every last one of them. One day another litter of kittens arrived, with a baby that was not right from the beginning, small and sickly, and although he did not die, he was not thriving either. It was finally ascertained that he was blind. Most farm cats had to work for their suppers, but Aunt Moggie would sneak this one scraps of food out of Uncle Pete's sight. He hated the crippled creature and vowed he would do away with him since he could not fend for himself. One cold, rainy Saturday—"town day" in the country back then because everyone went into town—Pete was in an especially foul humor and concentrated his petulance on the little blind kitten. He swore that he would stay behind that day and *kill that damned cat.*

When Aunt Moggie and the others returned a little earlier than expected, they rushed from the car to see if Pete had murdered the kitten. Pete was stone deaf and did not know his wife and the children were in the parlor until they were upon him. "There in the parlor," Jill Browne remembered, "before a roaring fire sat Uncle Pete in a rocking chair and on his lap was the little blind kitty, wrapped in a towel, eating a buttered biscuit and licking Pete's gnarled old hand. The squealing and laughing! They teased and teased him. Finally he could take it no more. He flew up out of his rocker, gently placing the kitten in his vacant seat, and stormed out of the house shouting, 'Well, hell, I was just gettin' the sumbitch warm before I drowned him!' The little blind kitty lived for years and years as the sole pet and dinner companion of my uncle Pete and nobody dared mention his death threats again."

Well, this gave one pause for thought, I suppose, the

confirmed backcountry cat tormenter turned soft. But it was not enough. So finally in my probing misgivings I sought out my son, David Rae, who as I have previously established had once so justly shared my predilection about dogs versus cats, but who himself had crossed that emphatic divide because of a woman. We were sitting in the end zone bleachers at halftime of an Ole Miss-Vanderbilt game; I recall the Rebels were about two touchdowns ahead of that ignominious Nashville football factory, and in the lull I explained to him my quandary. Since he was to be the best man in the forthcoming wedding, I told him I expected the utmost scrupulousness. The Ole Miss band was on the field in front of us performing a blend of "Dixie" and "The Battle Hymn of the Republic," which would have brought tears to the eyes of a Massachusetts abolitionist. Under the circumstances my questions must have seemed a little prickly, but that was my mood:

"So tell me about cats," I asked. "What are the differences between cats and dogs?"

"Well, cats are self-sufficient. They can take care of themselves. You don't have to bother with them. They come and go as they please. You have to let 'em be. If you want a good, loyal, generous cat you just have to let him be himself. I've found that every cat has a different, distinctive personality. Our cat Jewel is very stately and dignified, and Phoebe is a stray who's very adventurous and gets into play fights all the time."

"So they don't really need humans."

"Yeah, they do need us."

This was no help at all. "They can't eat off frogs all the time, can they?"

"Well, they could. I guess it's a delicate balance. Of course, it all depends on the cat too."

"Are cats smart?" I persisted.

"Oh, I think cats can be very smart."

"Are they as smart as dogs?"

"They sure can be."

"In what way, for God's sake?"

"Well, they're just . . . cats are predators, it's their jungle background. Dogs aren't predators. Cats catch things. They catch mice, squirrels, rabbits, bats—"

"*Bats?*"

"One of my cats in Minnesota once caught a bat. They'll bring you these animals as gifts, and you are to reward them."

"I wouldn't reward anybody for bringing me a bat." I guess I should have quoted here *Alice in Wonderland.* "Do cats eat bats? . . . Do bats eat cats?"

"Just pat them on the head and say 'Good job,' unless they bring you, say, a live rabbit. You've got to take it out of their mouths and let the rabbit go. This will befuddle them, because they thought they were bringing you this rabbit to show off their prowess as hunters."

Next the new feline savant began talking about how affectionate cats are, and that they show their affection in subtle ways. "They become part of your family, they entertain you, they comfort you." He continued: "A lot of people don't let their cats go outside, and I think that's wrong. Just let a cat be a cat, and that means let them claw the furniture and let them claw the rug. Modie spends most of his time outdoors. We put in a little cat door for him."

"*A cat door?*"

"Yeah, we put in a cat door for him."

So what he was trying to say, I suggested, is that cats could never be like dogs.

"Of course not. They're not as big, they behave

28

differently, but they're cleaner, they clean themselves and take care of themselves. You don't have to bathe them. They're in charge of their own hygiene, so you don't have to worry about them smelling. And they'll amuse you as much as dogs by the silly things they do. They provide you with comic relief. Modie, for instance, once got into a vat of grease."

"Hot grease?"

"No, not hot grease, but he looked like a big rat. All his fur was slicked back. We had to take him to a vet. Fortunately it was a Saturday and the groomer was there, and they used two boxes of cornstarch to absorb the grease, and he smelled like a doughnut for about a week."

"Well, you'd never have a problem like that with a dog."

"Oh, yeah? Didn't you once tell me your dog Skip got sprayed by a skunk and you and my grandfather had to bathe him in tomato juice?"

"You've got a good memory," I said.

CHAPTER 4

ALONG COMES SPIT MCGEE

IT WAS CHRISTMAS IN DIXIE, STILL MONTHS BEFORE our wedding. My future stepson Graham was then in high school and had a girlfriend named Savannah. Savannah was cruising along old Highway 51 north of Jackson one afternoon when she sighted a little starving, abandoned kitten in a ditch. She got out and put her in the car and took her home. When Graham saw the kitten, he suggested Savannah let him give it to his mother for a Christmas surprise. She liked the idea. Neither of them checked this out with me, I can tell you.

Graham and his mother dwelled at the time in a house on Northside Drive in Jackson in a neighborhood built up right after World War II, so that all the side streets were named after war sites. This house was at the intersection of Northside and Normandy, a homey domicile with rambling rooms and a big fireplace and a good back porch and lawn. The three of us had decorated a tall fresh Mississippi cedar with old family angels and Santas and reindeer and lights, which twinkled from the pungent branches.

It was late on Christmas Eve. We were sitting in the room near the tree, with a substantial number of presents around it. Nat King Cole's "I'll Be Home for Christmas" was on the stereo, or maybe it was Bing Crosby's "O Come All Ye Faithful." Suddenly, as if on cue, there was an odd rustling from the rear of the tree. And then tentatively stepping out over the packages into view was a tiny pure-white kitten with a red Yuletide ribbon around its neck.

"How did *he* get in here?" I heard myself exclaiming.

"It's a *she*," Graham said. "It's for you, Mom."

The kitten looked a little intimidated, which was precisely the way I felt in that moment. Although Savannah and Graham had fed and bathed her, she was a scrawny thing. But when my future spouse saw her, her features became flushed and joyous. Never had I seen such a happy female. She immediately swept the creature into her arms and embraced her. Then the kitten jumped onto the floor, ran back under the tree, and immediately shimmied up the main trunk. Christmas balls and angels crashed to the floor. Cedar trees are very dense, especially those strung with lights and ornaments. There was no way to coax her down; she would only climb farther up the tree. She was obviously going to come down when she was good and damned ready. "Just don't pay any attention to her and she'll come down sooner or later," JoAnne instructed. So we didn't, and that is precisely what she did.

It was a critical moment in my life, and by God I knew it. I left the room with the cat still in the tree and went outside to get some air. Only a couple of days before I had seen on TV a movie about one of my boyhood World

31

War II heroes, Admiral "Bull" Halsey, who when asked about his fluctuating strategies during the Battle of Guadalcanal replied, "It's not so much that you change your mind as that you go in a different direction." Well, it was Christmas, after all. I promised myself to at least give it a civilized try. I took a deep breath and went back inside.

On Christmas morning the little kitten was lapping milk from a bowl on the floor. She turned and looked at me, and I looked back at her. It was the genesis of a most unfamiliar relationship. Of course I did not know it then, but she would someday be the mother of Spit McGee.

The Cat Woman said she would allow me to name the kitten. I knew this was a craven bribe, but I named her Rivers Applewhite after the little girl I grew up with and wrote about, the one that Old Skip and I were both in love with. Perhaps the name itself would help me tolerate the unwarranted Christmas cat.

So now we had a Rivers Applewhite. She was an enigma to me. She was, as I have reported, absolutely white, with singular dark brown eyes. She was also very resilient and temperamental, and in her early days in that house kept testing me, as if I were unworthy of her. I tried not to pay her much mind, but she kept doing exasperating things that I was unable to ignore. She would perch silently on the rafters of the den, for example, then without warning leap down at me and land next to me on the sofa, thus scaring me witless. Mostly she would just sit and stare at me with her cantankerous, knowing eyes. What did she *know*? I certainly had no idea. She was exceedingly fast, and sometimes out of whatever motive she mindlessly sprinted through the dwelling with the velocity of a Jackie Joyner-Kersee. She was always hiding. The house was not of San Simeon proportions, but her hiding places were multifold and uncanny: under the kitchen sink, all the chairs and sofas and beds, in my shoes, and once even in the fireplace when it was not in use—what that did to a white cat is easy to imagine—and on the wall-length bookshelves. One day, after being missing for a couple of hours, we discovered her wedged between *The Brothers Karamazov* and *Down and Out in London and Paris*. As part of the Cat Woman's later confessional, she said: "Since she was a Christmas surprise, I didn't have an opportunity to think about how you'd react to her. And I'll bet neither did you. And how could I disappoint Graham and Savannah? I simply had to figure out a way to work her into our relationship and hope you'd go along with it. I never considered that you wouldn't."

Rivers obviously was drawn to my fiancée but mainly treated me on the scale of a ratty indentured servant just off steerage from eighteenth-century Liverpool. To put it mildly, I did not trust her very much, even on those winter nights she spent drowsily in front of the fireplace, tame as could be.

The first real test came a week or so after Christmas and was a trying one. We had enlisted my other future stepson, Gibson, to help me move out of my bungalow at Ole Miss and to bring all my possessions back to Jackson. The Cat Woman insisted we take Rivers Applewhite with us. She did not like it one bit. It was a three-hour drive to Oxford, and she whined and screamed and walked every inch of the car and on the car seats and under the car seats and on our necks. Once between Coffeeville and Water Valley she jumped onto my head and almost caused me to lose control of my clanking Dodge. "That cat is driving me crazy!" I shouted. I suggested we stop at a pharmacy and get her a high-powered sedative, something that would knock her out cold, or for that matter forever. But

33

somehow she finally settled down and we made it to our destination.

Once we arrived at my old place on Faculty Row, she was completely at home. Against all odds she immediately began to conduct herself with an unexpected decency. She took a place on the back of my big sofa and spent the next few days gazing out the window at the happenings on the street outside. The spirit of my noble departed Labrador, Pete, pervaded the house: the corners where he slumbered, his own personal woolen carpet in front of the fireplace, the spot in the dining room where he reclined as I wrote my stories. At any moment I expected him to come in the back door and leap up at me and lick my nose, then explore his familiar territory until against all reasonable justice he discovered a *cat* on his old premises. That might have sent him back to his grave. I was consumed with guilt when I used Pete's old food platter to put down cat food. It is always melancholy to move away forever from a place where you have dwelled for a very long time, for the past accumulates on you in fading mementos, documents and letters and photographs, reminders of the mortal days, and it is particularly trying to gather up these haunting artifacts of temporality with a cat looking at you. *What have I gotten myself into, Pete?*

I had to concede that Rivers was very smart. She could figure things out by herself. She soon determined that I did not have a clue about how to deal with her. I guess I just treated her as if she were a dog in cat's clothing, giving her sturdy slaps of affection, from which she would promptly run away. When I dumped whole cans of cat food onto her dish she would take a bite or two and contemptuously walk off. I saved huge hunks of meat and bones from my plate and put them down for her, and some sliced bologna—had not my dog Skip liked bologna?—and she ignored them all. She would not come when I called her or clapped my hands vigorously to get her attention or beat on the sofa for her to sit beside me. When I picked her up, she would not stay with me. Why could she not at least show even the most modest indications that she was happy to see me and to greet me when I was gone for several days? This puzzled and angered me. "Cats ain't dogs," I would shout accusingly at the Cat Woman.

This cat seemed basically a maverick, a loner, as I had always judged cats to be. There was a haughtiness to her, a demeanor of aristocracy that contradicted her incontrovertible Highway 51 ancestry. As she began to grow up, I also had to admit that she was pretty. She was an immaculate self-groomer and would spend interminable moments licking her paws and fur and tail. She was strange. Sometimes to see her reaction I would call out her name. Most of the time she would sit there disregarding me, but every now and again she would turn and acknowledge my call with lazy, dreamy eyes—ennui eyes: *What do you want?*

Nonetheless as I watched Rivers grow into a graceful, elegant young cat, I began to suspect she was more deep and subtle than I had supposed. I read at the Cat Woman's urging the exotic fairy tale "The White Cat," which the Mississippi artist Walter Anderson had interpreted in splendid block prints and which my friend Ellen Douglas had retold in her book *The Magic Carpet and Other Tales.* Despite her detached ways, Rivers could have been the magical cat princess whom the king's youngest son fell in love with.

She had the instincts of the huntress, as I had indeed been forewarned about cats, and warily stalked our

35

backyard on stealthy paws seeking things out. Sometimes she sharpened her claws on the bark of trees. I watched from afar as she scooted up these trees to their remotest branches, as if she were practicing what to do if something came after her. No one was teaching her these things; she just did them. The first time she came in the house with a lizard in her mouth, I was tempted to contact the lizard department of the humane society. This was a vicinity of squirrels, and she chased them incessantly with no success.

Since she was being well fed, she was fattening up and growing. One night something unforeseen happened. I was sitting in a chair reading a book when she suddenly leapt into my lap and began purring. She extended her paws and kneaded them on my legs. She began licking my fingers, surprising me not only by the intimacy of her action but by the sharp-razor feel of her tiny tongue. Did she think I was her *mother?* Or was she flirting with me? This was a new experience, a cat sitting in *my* lap and purring at *me.* Was something happening to me? We lived in a neighborhood with yards and trees, where cats could be indoors and outdoors. I began to worry that on her explorations outside the house she might get run over. I discovered myself standing on the back porch waiting for her to return.

Beyond a certain age a kitten grows up quickly. The following April, we noticed that her stomach was beginning to bulge. Surely she was not *pregnant;* she was still just a kitten, only five or six months old. I could hardly believe it: she was indeed with child. She would be a child mother, or at best a teenaged mother. "White trash!" I yelled at her.

Her conduct and demeanor now affected me, however. She became more affectionate toward me. There was a vulnerability to her, a warmth that I had never thought possible with cats. Could this have been an old, atavistic association with time itself? One afternoon I gazed at her for the longest moments as she rested on an ironing board on the back porch in the bedappled sunshine. Her tiny leonine eyes were aglow: she was *expecting* something. Occasionally she would awaken and gently lick her burgeoning belly. At other times I observed her as she searched the house for more secretive places to sleep.

The days went by. We were now well into May, in the flowering of the great Deep Southern springtime.

We knew Rivers's childbirth was imminent but did not know precisely when it would be. I found myself a little worried about this forthcoming event. This bizarre little cat had somehow, despite my reluctance, become at least an oblique part of my life, and I started quizzing JoAnne about the mechanics of cat-birthing. The Cat Woman did not seem to give it a thought. Most of her life, she reminded me, she had had at least one mother cat who had kittens every year and that when the time came the cat always went off by herself somewhere—usually to a closet, sometimes under a bed or in an outside storage room—and had the kittens. The Cat Woman never knew precisely when to expect this and never did much in the way of preparation. This seemed a fairly cavalier attitude to me. All the dogs of my life had been males, so I had had no experience with dog births, either. With her previous cats JoAnne used to just put some old towels or sheets or T-shirts in a little flat box in a small area in the back of a closet and show it to the expectant mother. If the cat liked the spot she would use that as her birthing bed, but if this did not suit her she would find her own space and make her own bed. She tried to explain that Rivers Applewhite would know instinctively what to do, but I was not convinced. "She's too young," I said, "not even a teenager yet." So we made places in every closet and dark nook and under every bed. The Mayo Clinic could not have done better.

As the delivery date approached David Rae was visiting from Minneapolis and we had a dinner party for him and some of his Jackson friends. Everyone was petting Rivers and predicting when she would deliver. The group left around midnight. Shortly after that, catastrophic things began to transpire.

This would become one of the memorable happenings of my life. I was sitting at the dining room table while JoAnne cleared the dishes. Suddenly Rivers began moaning and crying and running inanely from room to room. We tried to calm her down, but she refused to be pacified. One moment she would hide under a bed, the next in one of the closets. Every five minutes or so she would repeat the routine. This went on time and again. I was already a nervous wreck. How had I gotten into this? JoAnne decided something was badly wrong and telephoned the all-night emergency animal clinic, As I trailed Rivers in her frenetic scrambles, I could hear JoAnne describing what was going on and asking if a cat ever needed a cesarean or if she might not instinctively know how to give birth. The emergency vet said both were possible but to give her more time before we brought her in.

Soon after the phone call, Rivers started her dervish again. But this time as I followed her dashing from the bedroom closet into the dining room she did something that nothing whatever in my entire existence had remotely prepared me for. She flung from her insides onto the floor a slimy gray thing with no head or eyes or nose or ears or tail! "Oh, my God!" JoAnne shouted. "She's had a deformed baby! Or maybe it's premature?" Rivers lurched nearby as I squeamishly hovered over the formless blob, which resembled nothing if not the pulsating pods in the old movie *Invasion of the Body Snatchers.* Once again JoAnne phoned the emergency vet and described the situation. He calmly suggested that perhaps the amniotic sac was still in place on the newly born kitten. He proceeded to give her exact directions on what to do. With the telephone cord pulled out to its fullest length, she began relaying the instructions to me.

Indulge me, reader, to interject here that when I was growing up, people expected me to be a medical doctor—that was what all bright Southern boys were supposed to aspire to then, but I would not for a nonce so much as think of it, and for one very sound reason: I hated the sight of blood. And here I was at 2 A.M. in a house in Jackson, Mississippi, expected to deliver a cat. "I don't know nothin' about birthin' cats," I heard myself saying. But there was scant choice.

"Get some paper towels," the vet's orders were repeated to me. "Rub the thing up and down and over and over." I proceeded to do so. After a minute or more of this, beneath the oozing blood I began to see ears and a nose and a head—a little cat, a little *white* cat.

"Continue rubbing! This is what the mother should be doing by licking the kitten!" So I rubbed and rubbed.

"Rub it hard on the back to help it breathe! *Pat! Pat!*" This went on endlessly. "Live, kid, live!" I yelled. And, by God, it began breathing deeply and making faint noises and moving its mouth.

Somehow all of this seemed to calm Rivers Applewhite, and she sedately retreated into the bedroom closet again and gave birth to another one—a yellow one. She did everything right this time. I took the little white one in my arms and gently put it in there with her. Then she delivered another white one and a little black-and-white one all by herself.

I would give the first little white one, whose life I had saved, the name Spit McGee.

The name derived from a character in a children's book I once wrote. Spit was a mischievous and resourceful boy who could spit farther than anyone else in the whole town. This is how I described him in that book:

Spit lived in the swamps, and he was a hunter and fisherman. Foxie Tompkins might bring an apple to school for the teacher, but not Spit. If he brought her anything it would be a catfish, or a dead squirrel for frying. Rivers Applewhite would often be the recipient of the most beautiful wild swamp flowers, which Spit brought into town in the spring. One day during recess Spit reached into his pockets and pulled out a dead grubworm, a live boll weevil, a wad of chewed-up bubble gum, four leaves of poison ivy which he said he was not allergic to, two shotgun shells, a small turtle, a rusty fish hook, the feather from a wild turkey, a minnow, the shrunken head of a chipmunk, and a slice of bacon.

And with his namesake begins a new chapter in this vainglorious writer's life.

Without wishing to sound histrionic, the birth of Spit and his three siblings evoked for me a reserve of continuity, of the generations, of life passing on life, of the cycles. By the second day it was obvious that Rivers, so poignantly and recently a kitten herself, was making a good little mother, her maternal instincts as strong as those of the backyard huntress.

Although the kittens' eyes would remain closed for ten

40

days or so, when they were only hours old they were active and curious. The white female kitten we named Savannah, after my stepson's girlfriend who had rescued Rivers from the ditch on Highway 51. She looked bigger and healthier than Spit. We named the yellow one Peewee after a childhood chum of mine, and the black-and-white one Jimmy Carter for regional reasons. Any good mother loves and fears for her young, and I noted how Rivers would take the kittens with her mouth around the backs of their necks and hide them somewhere from time to time, as if she felt incipient dangers lurking for them. Once she had them settled somewhere, she was almost like a generic time clock. She would nurse them and watch over them, and about every two and a half hours as they slept together in a furry mass she would emerge to eat, relax, lie outside in the sunshine—then soon metronomically return to them again.

Then we discovered that Rivers and the kittens had fleas. This turned out to be a wicked flea year in Jackson, which happens every now and then, and the kittens had more than their share. JoAnne called the vet for information about what to do. Just powder them with another kind of flea powder, the vet advised, and gave a brand name. So we began bringing the kittens out one by one and lavishing them with flea powder. Each time we did this, Rivers would move the kittens to another hiding place. After three or four of these moves, she located a spot we could not find. For days we would see her sneak through a cabinet in the basement, but search as we did we could not locate the sequestered kittens. She began spending more time away from them, and we became anguished. Friends came and helped us look, but the kittens had vanished.

Finally, we found her hiding place under the house. I

crawled under there and looked at them. Only one of the kittens was alive—one of the white ones. I surmised it was Savannah, since little Spit had been so tiny to begin with. But she was alive just barely, only a wisp of life lingering, as if she would expire at any moment. I put her in my arms and we took her to the car to rush her to the animal emergency clinic.

JoAnne drove the three miles to the clinic. To allow the stricken kitten to breathe better, I held her up on the dashboard. She was only slightly bigger than the palm of my hand. She hardly could move there. But she extended her paws toward me, as if she desperately wanted to live, bobbing her head lightly back and forth. At the destination JoAnne was too distraught to leave the car. I took the kitten inside.

The animal nurse on duty examined the patient and declared her technically dead. Nothing could be done, she said. But then the veterinarian came in, whose name was Dr. Majure. He looked over the woebegone little creature more closely. "There's hope," he said. "We've got a cat who gives blood transfusions to sick kittens." They called him Clinic Cat and he had already saved several kittens. He was two years old, weighed sixteen pounds, and had Type B blood, he said, the preferred type for cat transfusions.

"Your kitten's dying of anemia. Leave him here overnight. We'll fetch Clinic Cat. There's a chance we can save him. I can't promise. Come back in the morning."

I was about to leave, but tarried at the door. "Did I hear you say *him*? My cat?"

"Sure. He's a male."

In the car I told JoAnne about the projected transfusion, then: "But it's not Savannah. It's Spit McGee."

42

I spent a restless night, consumed with worry for the dying Spit. With trepidation I returned the next day. The vet brought him out to me. "He's going to be okay. The little fellow didn't want to die." The transformation from the previous night was miraculous. His eyes were bright and he moved about vigorously in the arms of the vet. "This is going to be a good cat, this boy," he surmised. "This is going to be a *bad* cat. See what I've noticed? He's got one blue eye and one golden eye. That's a good sign. And look who's here." A huge, furry cat with Siamese eyes and eclectic orange colors strolled into the room. I knew who this was without asking. "Thank you, Clinic Cat," I said.

CHAPTER 5

"CATS AIN'T DOGS"

WITH THE SURVIVAL OF SPIT MCGEE I WOULD BECOME against all past injunctions a cat-watcher, observing his curious development from a kitten on. And I guess almost from the start the central threat in our relationship was trying to figure each other out: a human being and a cat across the great warm-blooded mammal chasm.

Normally a kitten depends on his mother's milk for about seven weeks. But after the death of the three others in the litter, Rivers Applewhite was for a time remote and confused and refused to nurse the surviving infant. The trustworthy Dr. Majure immediately prescribed Milk for Motherless Kittens, which is available in stores, and also vitamin pills to fight any recurrence of the dreaded anemia. The Cat Woman and I would feed him the survivor milk with a dropper.

He was now about three weeks old and began investigating the household on wavering but serviceable legs. Yet he always managed to return to me, to crawl onto my feet and look up at me. Sometimes he would be playful, reaching out toward me with his paws; at others, sphinxlike, staring silently at me with his big luminous eyes. What creature is this? he seemed to be saying of me. I was not sure who he was either. When I put him in my lap, he would try to embrace me with his paws, just as my dog Skip once did as a puppy. But sometimes he would withdraw and start looking at me again, a look of near bottomless intensity. This was discombobulating.

He did indeed have one blue eye and one golden one, which never failed to intrigue visitors. The golden eye sometimes changed shades, from light brown to dark brown and back to golden again, and I could not understand the reason for these fluctuating gradations. The old wisdom, someone tried to explain to me, was that a cat with two different-colored eyes is born deaf. "I will be deafer than the blue-eyed cat," I remember Tennyson had written in *Idylls of the King,* but he had not taken into account the more storied jeremiad, obviously inaccurate, about the two-colored eyes—and in any case with Spit nothing patently could have been further from the truth. Spit's ears were in constant movement, turned to a train's whistle half a mile away, or the shouts of neighborhood children ineffably at play, or the bark of faraway dogs. I would always answer to those who reiterated this dog-eared adage under the guise of expertise that Spit's auditory sense was so impeccable that he could pick up dinner conversations in Memphis two hundred miles away.

I was interested in the way he groomed himself after his meals of Motherless Milk and vitamins, a complicated routine as I had earlier seen with his mother, Rivers, that followed an almost ritualized pattern, beginning with his licking his lips and ending later by his licking the whole length of his tail. I was also mystified by the way he seemed to gesture and talk to me with his tail, esoteric propulsions that appeared to signify something—what, I did not know. I liked to examine his paws, which were intricate and mysterious to me, and I watched the movements too of his whiskers, slowly back and forth in one motion and fast and agitated in the next. What kind of inborn signal was this?

I was engaged in writing a book, on William Faulkner, no less, and had taken a room to finish it in an erstwhile and flamboyant Jackson institution called the Sun-N-Sand Motel, just down from the state capitol. I would live in the Sun-N-Sand until the Cat Woman and I got married, although I spent a great deal of time in the house at Northside and Normandy. The physiognomy and decor of the Sun-N-Sand were straight out of the 1950s, and since numerous members of the state legislature rented rooms here, it had been famous for many years for its egregious political wheelings and dealings, not to mention its secretive trysts. In the shadowy bar with Patsy Cline and Hank Williams and Loretta Lynn on the jukebox, or in the dining room at breakfast, the pols more or less passed that day's legislation, merely to be formalized later on the floors of the capitol. "If Washington, D.C., had a Sun-N-Sand," one of that institution's regular denizens said to young Spit and me in our room one day, "with political enemies cooperatin' so good, they'd get along a lot better up there."

Every afternoon I drove Spit down to the Sun-N-Sand to keep me company while I worked, and I always made sure to bring the vitamin pills and the Milk for Motherless Kittens with me. He was about a month old at the time and had become steadfastly active. I usually let him roam the motel room as he wished, and he slowly began exploring every piece of furniture, every interior precipice,

46

every nook and cranny. I had index cards arranged in chronological stacks on the bed behind my worktable, which faced a sizeable plate-glass window with a vista onto the parking lot and the dome of the capitol building beyond, and the main problem was that in his explorations Spit would scratch ponderously up onto the bed—he was much too young then for his later prodigious leaps—and proceed to disarrange my index cards. (When the book was subsequently published, one zealous Yankee critic, a neo -existentialist Marxist from the Upper West Side of New York City, I think, or maybe it was Berkeley, criticized the chronology of the concluding chapters, for which I could only blame the callow Spit McGee for knocking down my index cards.) He also had an inclination for climbing with his already raspy-sharp claws onto my table, poking his nose into the pages I was working on, and sometimes even sitting down on my writing hand, an intrusiveness of his that as time progressed would never once leave him, and for which no mutual compromise ever succeeded. When he became too obstreperous in this regard I devised a plan. I was reluctant to shut him up in the bathroom, so with all the books sprawled around everywhere I constructed a fairly imposing rectangular pen and put him in there from time to time. He did not like this very much, and was always trying to escape. Once he shimmied up the stack of books on one side of the pen, knocked down *The Sound and the Fury* and *Absalom! Absalom!* with his nose and paws, and accomplished his deliverance, after which I stacked the books higher and made the arrangement secure as Alcatraz.

Much of the time, however, especially after I had given him his formula milk, he would sleep on my worktable. When he awakened, he would spend long moments gazing out the window at the dome of the capitol, or at the motel passersby, or at the Sun-N-Sand's resident cat, a big fat yellow cat with chartreuse eyes about sixteen times larger than my diminutive companion, who often would jump onto the window ledge outside and silently stare back in at Spit.

In late afternoons I would sometimes take a brief sabbatical and we would be visited by a plethora of talkative souls of all political persuasions, roughly 180 degrees along the entire political spectrum, especially the state legislators, who developed a fondness for the adventurous kitten. One of them, who had had some sour-mash whiskey in the Sun-N-Sand bar, tried to feed him from a can of Copenhagen snuff. Once even the senior U.S. senator Mr. Thad Cochran dropped in, and asked if writers usually wrote in the company of cats. Our neighbor in the adjoining room was Aaron Henry, the black civil rights leader and state legislator, and he would come by and try to feed Spit peanuts and potato chips. Two identical male twins, age about eighty, who dwelled permanently in a nearby room and could often be seen through their window stretched out on the floor sound asleep, several times offered me twenty dollars for Spit. So you have some notion of the kind of habitat the two of us frequented daily for well over a month. I sometimes wonder nowadays if Spit remembers those times, because he definitely began his growing up there.

As my regard for him and my heightening interest in all phases of his conduct grew, several times I caught myself unconsciously addressing him as "Skip," or "Pete." I could not believe myself for doing this. How could I have fathomed then how much I would grow to love him?

I would be sitting in my chair at the house at Northside

and Normandy and his habit was to approach the chair, position himself between my feet and look up longingly at me. Then he would climb my leg into my lap. A dozen or more times a night he would do this. That was when I started trying seriously to talk to him, as he sat in my lap on these evenings. I would talk to him about my dogs Skip and Pete, or what I had done that day, or an Atlanta Braves game I was watching on TV, and he would stare at me, and blink his eyes, and make the incomprehensible movements of his tail and whiskers. This might suggest how radically far I had come, to be actually trying to converse with a kitten.

Then one night after playing outdoors, he did not come home. He was gone for several hours. I had read somewhere of the high mortality rates of kittens and young cats: killed by dogs, run over, lost far from home, wounded by sadistic Homo sapiens. We had purposefully decided to let him, as with his mother, Rivers Applewhite, go outdoors on his own, and now I was disturbed by that decision. He had almost died at birth, and then most certainly would have done so two weeks later had it not been for Clinic Cat, and this now was the third of a succession of traumas we would have with him over time. I walked from house to house in the neighborhood. I got in the car and roamed the vicinity looking for him. I remembered with lucid anathema how Skip had disappeared in Yazoo City, Mississippi, in 1944, and Pete in Oxford, Mississippi, in 1982, and I wanted none of that now. When I was getting down to writing about this, the Cat Woman reminded me of the episode in searing particulars: "You wouldn't speak to me. You told me it was my fault because I'd gotten you involved with a damned cat and you couldn't deal with him. You said you didn't begin to understand cats and were sick and tired of

49

them. You closed yourself in your room. Just like anytime anything happened to one of our cats later on, you were *nuts*. And you, the cat hater! We'd given up on Spit. Late that night, we were crying and discussing all the details of his short little life."

And then, right in that instant, we heard a faint noise outside the front window. It sounded like *meeow*. I went to the window. And there was Spit McGee.

Cat specialists testify that at about five weeks kittens have their own well-developed personalities, and at two months they start becoming more solitary, and I have found this to be approximately correct. Spit certainly had arrived at a personality: cranky, playful, unpredictable, smart, ornery, reflective, and eventually now he would be more and more on his own.

I have specified that after the death of her three other kittens and the near demise of the sole survivor, Rivers became for a time quirky and withdrawn, and, of all the cats we would have, she would be by far the most complicated, having to do in some measure, perhaps, with her Highway 51 genesis. Her later relationships with the grown-up Spit and others of our subsequent cats would be as complex as any human ones I had ever seen, but that is in the future. Now, however, with Spit McGee, she began to return to certain maternal obligations.

I started to notice Spit watching her more closely, the way she moved and listened and observed and behaved herself. In our backyard in late afternoons and early evenings I was spellbound to see her consciously teaching things to him: how to sharpen his claws by scratching them on the bark of trees, for instance, or how to climb the trunks of trees into the overhead branches, and Spit would studiously watch her and then try to emulate her.

50

Suddenly she would become utterly still and with a muted gaze peer suspiciously into the distance, and Spit's eyes would follow hers: two dogs on a leash, followed by the owner. And then, moments later, he would track again her movements as she stalked in the grass and weeds, on serpentine tiptoes, body low to the ground, searching for small creatures, bringing back to him a minuscule mouse or lizard or insect for his own private perusal, and soon I would see him in his own subtle searchings. Sitting on the back porch in the broiling summer nights I could not take my sight away from these atavistic entertainments. I marveled at how the two of them got around so well in the impenetrable darkness, their probing eyes like glowing circles, afraid of nothing, looking for everything.

Spit was becoming a figure of unusual habitudes, one of these being that he often slept on his back with all four legs sticking straight up. There he would be, drowsing in the sunshine in the backyard, and looking for all the world like a very miniature Moby Dick without harpoons sticking out of him. I more or less took this peculiarity of his for granted—what did I know?—until my fiancée and other cat authorities informed me that they had almost never seen a cat sleep in such an idiosyncratic posture, and he would carry this into adulthood. Cold, gloomy weather invariably affected Spit McGee, and the more purple and drizzly the overhanging heavens the deeper and more seriously he slumbered. On frigid winter days at the first sight of a roaring fire in the fireplace he would walk up toward that fire, sniff around a little, and then with an audible sigh collapse on his back, extend his paws in the air, and stay there. "That's a very special cat," people would say. "He's inherited *something*."

Another of his notable characteristics was the way he walked. He not so much walked as *glided,* with a sort of jaunty athletic rhythm to his hips, and he was ever so slightly bowlegged, like distinguished running backs sometimes are. In my later inquiries at the Welty Library I picked up somewhere that cats do not merely walk on their toes, but unlike horses and dogs they both walk and run by first moving the front and back legs on one side, then the front and back legs on the *other* side, and that only giraffes and camels and cats move in this way. That in itself explained something to me about Spit's running ability, Do any of you remember the great running back Jim Brown of the Syracuse Orangemen and later the Cleveland Browns, how indolent he looked when he got up after being tackled, and even lazier when he came out of the huddle, and then when they gave him the football how he pumped his legs and seemed to progress at the approximate acceleration of sound? Well, that is the way Spit began to appear to me when, on awakening from a mid-afternoon's siesta, he aimlessly walked around a little, snooped some in the grass, then when something drew his attention he started galloping off as nimbly as Jim Brown ever had. (In these intimate observations, I actually began to concede that Spit could have outrun Old Skip, even if Skip *did* hold the world's mark for fox terriers in the 100-yard dash.) That was when I began to consider Spit an athlete.

Because of that, and of my background with cerebral and agile dogs, I concluded to teach him specific things. One entire afternoon, for example, I was determined to get him to approach me when I said, *"Come here!"* I repeated this about eight dozen times, punctuating this most sensible of commands by pulling him bodily toward me so he would get the idea. He looked at me with his two-pronged eyes as if I were deranged. Then there were the long sessions in which I tried to teach him to shake hands, to lie down, to roll over, to play dead. Several of the neighborhood children would watch this from beyond our backyard fence and laugh raucously at the sight of Spit walking away from me to sit on his haunches and examine me with his expressions of unmitigated disdain. Then, with my most pervasive recollections of Skip and Pete going after sticks, I tried my most earnest to get him to retrieve. For the larger part of a week I damned near threw my arm bone out of its socket tossing sticks for him, and only once did he even come close to responding, and this when he imperially strolled down to where a stick had landed, sniffed it for the most transient instant, and proceeded forthwith to climb the most convenient tree. "Cats ain't dogs!" I began to exclaim all over again, shouting it several times in the direction of the cynical neighborhood brats in the audience behind the fence, to which they guffawed more irreligiously than ever. Later I tried throwing a brand-new tennis ball for him. "*Go get it!*" I yelled, to which after only one throw he batted the ball around on the ground with his paws for a moment, then turned on his heels, strode into the house, and proceeded to fall fast asleep on top of the refrigerator. Sometimes the Cat Woman would watch these proceedings from the back porch, and more than once she laughed sacrilegiously the way the disrespectful kids always did. In fact, it seemed the only issue we ever argued over was that bedrock principle, indigenous to my very heritage itself, of why cats do not behave like dogs.

"Why doesn't he do what I tell him to do?" I asked her in my honest exasperation.

"Because it isn't his idea," she replied.

Along about then, I decided that because of the way Spit was making fun of me I had better do a little research on cats, not so much in a scholarly, monkish manner but in the more straightforward, utilitarian interests of getting along with him. I went down to the Eudora Welty Public Library on North State Street in Jackson to see what they had. A matronly researcher who told me she herself lived with three highly aristocratic cats—a Persian, a Manx, and a Siamese—provided me a few books and a couple of videotapes. "Cats are the world's most inscrutable animals," she said to me as I departed, a little bitingly, I sensed, "and sadly misunderstood." And with that she wished me an ironic Godspeed.

I will cite only the high points. Do any of you know that dogs have been domesticated for twelve thousand years, and cats for only five thousand? I did not. Or that cats first came to America on the *Mayflower?* Why the *Mayflower?* one might ask. To establish a well-bred cat genealogy of which the DAR itself might someday be titillated? No, to kill rats.

From that august authority the *Encyclopaedia Britannica,* I learned that before their domestication, cats, unlike dogs, who roamed together in packs, were pretty much self-sufficient. Dogs had easily transferred their allegiances from the leaders of their packs to their human masters, but cats had not made the transformation to domestication so readily. From my empirical studies of Rivers Applewhite and Spit McGee, that was something I could agree with.

And here are some figures that attracted me. About sixty million cats presently live in nearly 30 percent of American households, and pet cats outnumber dogs in the Great Republic by almost two to one. The bookish consensus, however, was that more people dislike cats than dislike dogs and that although there is much evidence that women in general like cats and men like dogs, that may be changing. Cats first appeared about seven million years ago and there has been very little physical change in them into contemporary times. And here is one for you: a cat's physiognomic composition is such that he has 290 bones and 517 muscles; also, his brain, though small in dimension, is with the exception of the ape's the most highly developed on the evolutionary scale and the one most similar to the human brain. One arcane statistic, allegedly testifying to the popularity of cats and their ancestry, leapt out at me: in Division IA and IAA of the National Collegiate Athletic Association, no fewer than *nine* American college and university athletic teams have the nickname "Wildcats" (often shortened to the more manageable "Cats"), while *twelve* have the moniker "Tigers." As a sports fan I was interested in this information to the point that the roster of these schools will comprise the one and only footnote you will be able to find in this entire volume.*

*The following are Wildcats: Arizona, Bethune-Cookman, Davidson, Kansas State, Kentucky, New Hampshire, Northwestern, Weber State, and Villanova. Tigers are: Auburn, Clemson, Grambling, Jackson State, LSU, Memphis, Missouri, Pacific, Princeton, Tennessee State, Texas Southern, and Towson State. Then there are the Bobcats of Montana State, Ohio, and Southwest Texas State, the Bearcats of Cincinnati, and the BearKats (spelled with a "k") of Sam Houston State. (I do not include on this list various Cougars, Leopards, and Panthers.) The combined cat family exceeds the dog family—with eleven Bulldogs, two Terriers, and one Greyhound—by a total of 26 to 14, and even doubles our national symbol, the Eagles (or in some instances Golden Eagles).

In this unsystematized delving I was also drawn to another arresting theory by one Mr. Michael J. Rosen about dogs and cats:

> Stories with dogs concern families, corroborations, communities and collective reconciliations; stories with cats concern independence, individual solitudes . . . separations and insights into personal and family identities. . . . Primarily, the cat is a character of being; the dog, a character of doing.

I judged this a fruitful insight to carry into my new and emphatic interrelation with Spit McGee.

The writings that afforded me in the broader scope the weighty substance I most desired, however, were by Mr. Cleveland Amory. I was drawn to them because I had once, years before, actually met Mr. Amory, and under uncommon circumstances. I had recently gone to work as a junior editor on a national magazine based in New York City when one afternoon a secretary rushed to my humble cubbyhole to report that some strange man was at that very moment beating up my boss, the editor in chief. I hastened to my superior's office to ascertain this to be correct. A large unkempt fellow was pummeling my editor in chief about the shoulders and head with a rolled-up umbrella. He had pretty much finished and turned to me as he was leaving. "Hello," he said, "Cleveland Amory's the name." I would learn that Mr. Amory, as a leader in the national anti-vivisectionist movement, which sought an end to the torture of cats in research laboratory experiments, had come to protest a recent article in the magazine that had taken sides with the vivisectionists, so naturally I was curious to read a few of the things Cleveland Amory himself had to say about cats.

In ancient India, and in Burma and Siam, he informed me, cats were highly venerated for guarding temples and for what was regarded as the transmigration of souls: it was widely believed the human soul was relived in the body of a cat before proceeding to perfection in the nether life. In Japan the cat had avid religious significance that went beyond its usefulness in dealing with the rats that were destroying the silkworm industry. In ancient China, cats were esteemed as bearers of good luck because they lived and worked under the auspices of the Hearth God. And the Chinese peasant, like the Egyptian, believed the glow of the cat's eyes chased away evil spirits. In ancient Egypt there were religious cat cults and temple worship of cats. So from all this I began to deduct that Spit McGee directly descended from illustrious and tenacious forebears.

In safe, sane Europe in the Middle Ages, however, Spit's predecessors fell on murky times. Unlike the salubrious respect given them in the East, in the West cats came to be considered the literal embodiments of the devil—sources of witchcraft, black magic, and voodoo. Cats were burned alive, and people were dismembered piece by piece, beginning first with their toes and proceeding gradually upward to all other appendages, and finally, mercifully hanged for helping ill or wounded cats. In the early American colonies, in fact, some two thousand accusations of witchcraft involving cats were upheld in the courts of law themselves. Everywhere the poor black cat had the worst of it—tortured and massacred even during ceremonial black masses. (And as for black cats, have you ever read a scarier story than Edgar Allan Poe's "The Black Cat," which kept me up with cold fright for two whole nights as a boy?) From my desultory readings, in fact, I was dutifully edified that cats over the ages have probably been the most exploited and mistreated of all animals (except, perhaps, I irreverently scribbled down, human beings?).

I gathered Spit McGee should judge himself fortunate, then, to be a modern American cat, born into an at least tentative and sanguine multiethnic democracy. As for other facts about his quintessential composition, Mr. Cleveland Amory reported a historic phenomenon that infatuated me more than anything else I was able to unearth in the entire Eudora Welty Public Library: namely, the exceptional regard in which white cats have been held through historical time. (The reader has been generously apprised by now that my cat Spit McGee is all white, and descended from an all-white mother whose genes must have been so strong that in her first litter she had two white kittens.) There is no solid evidence that white cats were held as mystical exceptions in the Dark Ages of cat hysteria, but once that era was over white cats were generally acknowledged as unique and significant cats. In areas of the Orient they were thought sacred: the Burmese called them the "immaculate" cats. White cats were court pets under Louis XV, then Queen Victoria, and both the Japanese and Chinese emperors, and in Siam white cats were carried in court processionals because the soul of a king's predecessor was thought to be embodied in them.

I confronted Spit McGee when he was perusing the backyard before I started trying him with sticks and tennis balls again. "Spit," I said, "do you know you're a relative of the Chinese Hearth God?" It did not seem to faze him.

The day finally came when the Cat Woman and I were married. It was a back porch ceremony with only family in attendance. From beyond the fence the neighborhood kids who had made jest of me for throwing sticks for the growing kitten watched, and Rivers Applewhite looked down from the apex branch of a tree. David Rae Morris as best man stood at my side. During the vows themselves I heard a rustling in the nearby bushes. Sensing something momentous, perhaps, which would forever be his wont, who should walk up the steps and stand on the other side of me but young Spit McGee? As he stood there, he ceremoniously looked up at me. *In sickness and in health, till death us do part* . . . I considered him in that instant my co-best man.

CHAPTER 6

UNFORESEEN HAZARDS

HAVE YOU EVER NOTICED THAT WHEN YOU CARE FOR somebody, sometimes you call him, or her, by different names? I have several nicknames for my wife, including, as you have certainly perceived, the Cat Woman. Since I was being drawn to Spit, I started also addressing him as "Spitty," "Spitter," "Spit McGee," and at times "McGee," "Mr. McGee," or "Gee." In his own good time he would respond to each, but with precious little haste. Either that or he would just ignore me as usual.

Sweet would not be an appropriate adjective for Spit, nor do I think he himself would for a moment expect it, for it was far too simplistic and would fail to take into account several of his more obstinate intrigues. As he grew up, for instance, he refined his disagreeable exercise of striking out at me with his paw whenever he wanted something of me, even if that was merely to rub his neck and ears. In my researches I had read somewhere that the physiology laboratory at no less than Oxford University had once conducted paw-preference tests on sixty cats and ascertained that the vast majority of them favored their left paw. With Spit this was not so, at least not totally: he

60

might make an egregious southpaw feint at me, but the main jab that followed was with his other paw, as swift and nefarious as any Muhammad Ali right cross. Until I learned by the precise glint in his dual-hued eyes when he was about to draw my attention in this formidable manner, and readied myself to outmaneuver him with an equally inconsiderate little thrust of my own to his exposed solar plexus, I retained a container of hydrogen peroxide at hand for the scratches.

Sweet not being the right word notwithstanding, his moods of affection were rapid and variable. On cold nights he snuggled next to me in the bed and nuzzled me with his nose. Sometimes he slumbered with his paw around my neck, the same one he might the next day try to jab me with. In such moments he smelled good, like dry, fresh powder. Once when he was about three months old I had a bout with pneumonia and had to take to my bed for several days. He seemed to sense something, because he almost never left me.

The communicative gestures of cats to humans, I was learning, were very peculiar. When Rivers Applewhite wanted to be fed in the early morning, or let out of the house, she would rattle the venetian blinds in our bedroom with her paws. Spit had two tactics: either to bite you gently on the nose, or if that did not work to retreat into the bathroom and knock things on the floor—tubes of toothpaste, bars of soap, bottles of shampoo and mouthwash, shaving kits, hairbrushes, anything he could find that would cause a suitable racket.

Strangely, unlike his mother and the other cats to follow in our life, he almost never meowed, but when he did so you had better pay attention, because there was something urgent that needed to be attended to. Then there was the language of his tail, which took me a long

61

time to comprehend. If his tail was moving sedately from side to side, that more likely than not signified that he was momentarily pleased with things as they were, and that he was more or less concentrating on something not particularly earth-shattering. If his tail oscillated between stressful movements and lethargic ones, that was usually a sign he could not make up his mind about something, such as whether he wanted to be let outside when it was cold or raining. Petulant movements back and forth meant one thing: he was angry as hell, and you had just as well find out why right now.

His dining habits were equally inexplicable to me. I was learning that cats eat more frequently than I ever expected, but when they are eating they do so delicately, almost contemplatively. Where Skip could devour several slices of bologna in an instant, and Pete could finish off a whole can of dog food in the time it may have taken you to read the preceding sentence, Spit took his own good time. His main diet consisted of canned cat food and dry food in different flavors, and when these had been left out too long he would bite me on the ankles to protest their unfreshness. Unlike Skip and Pete, he was attracted neither to chicken livers nor bologna nor parched peanuts, but frequently I saw him finishing the remnants of a chicken pot pie—as well as sardines, bacon, and roasted Cornish game hens. I myself considered milk and Coca-Cola the most underrated beverages in America, and Spit apparently agreed. He drank a lot of milk, and a little Coca-Cola on torpid summer days, and if I sliced for him the spicy cheese straws that are a specialty of Yazoo City, Mississippi, he would have a go at them also; once he even ate four Girl Scouts cookies I crumbled up for him. He was, in fact, a fool about cheese of all kinds except Camembert; ordinary yellow rat-trap cheese was his favorite. He even liked fresh boiled asparagus if this was garnished with grated Parmesan cheese. But the luxury he was taken with the most ever since his days as a growing kitten was, of all things, Gerber baby food strained turkey. I once bought a container of this strained turkey as little more than a lark to see what he thought of it and soon it became his number-one delicacy, and I would bring some home to him a couple of times a week. One afternoon in the Jitney Jungle I was tossing a few of these Gerber turkeys into the shopping cart when a handsome young blond woman named Julie who had been in my literature class at Ole Miss happened by. "Come on, Professor," she said. "Are you still having babies?" and when I told her whom they were for she shook her head disbelievingly and went right on by. Spit liked Gerber turkey so much, indeed, that he began to recognize the distinctive sharp metallic click the top to the container made when I twisted it off. I would be in the kitchen and he on the sofa in the den, perhaps, or even way out on the back porch, but when he heard that brassy echo he wasted no time at all in coming right toward it.

Cats, I would also determine, adore new things. When we got a picnic table for the backyard, that was the first item Spit went to, examining it, sniffing it out, sleeping on it. A pile of lumber brought in to repair an outside storage room became his roost for days—as well as something as humbling as a washtub or a lawn mower. If a visitor's car was in the driveway, he would climb it, walk around the top, and sniff it too. When David Rae arrived from Minneapolis, Spit spent long hours in the bed of his pickup truck. So too with new people. He could be a social creature, but only up to a point. When we had gatherings in our house, he would sometimes pick out someone he had never seen before to be friendly with.

63

I likewise began to notice his interest in, if you can believe it, the telephone. Sometimes when I was talking to someone on the phone he would leap onto the desk and sit next to me, as if he were trying to hear what was coming through the other end. Old Skip never did this, but Pete sometimes had. I would tell the person on the line to call out *Spit* several times, then put the receiver up to him, at which his eyes would brighten and both of his ears start twitching. He also would pause from time to time when someone was leaving a message on the answering machine and I was not picking up the telephone. I confess here to a storied distaste for responding to telephones under all circumstances, and have often been known to put them out of the way in ovens or refrigerators, and if I was standing there while someone was recording a message on the infernal gadget, Spit would often stare at me skeptically as if to say, "Is he going to answer it or not?"

Given this exotic caprice for wanting to listen in on telephone conversations when this seized his fancy, I recall one evening in those days when a well-known sportswriter friend of mine named Rick Cleveland, a big dog person who claimed Spit McGee the only cat he had ever tolerated or for that matter ever would, and I decided to play a telephone hoax. (I once asked Rick Cleveland why he tolerated Spit in this way above all cats, and he haltingly replied, "Well, I'm not so sure. It's his two different eyes. Also, he has character for a cat. For me I guess he's like a . . . dog.") The imperious personage David Duke, the Ku Kluxer and neo-Nazi, was running for governor of the neighboring state of Louisiana. It was election night, and the sportswriter stood by as I dialed the number of Mr. Duke's campaign headquarters in Baton Rouge. Immediately Spit jumped onto the desk and posted himself next to me.

A campaign receptionist answered. "David Duke headquarters," she said.

"Can we speak to Eva Braun, please?"

"Eva who?"

"Eva Braun."

"I don't know her. What's she look like?"

"She's a tall blond and looks Aryan."

"Hold on. I'll page her." I put the receiver to Spit's ear as for long moments it boomed, "Paging Eva Braun . . . paging Eva Braun," and his ears twitched more vehemently than they ever had. (This could not help but remind me of Skip in the World War II years, when he would leap onto and vehemently shake the scarecrow in the Victory garden in our backyard, which was a replica of Eva Braun's boyfriend Hitler. I never knew a dog so down on Hitler.)

In this attenuated catalog of Spit's sharpening practices, I must also stress his innate wariness of dogs of all kinds. There would later be exceptions to this, but for now he kept a circumspect eye out for all dogs. Sitting on the dining room table and looking out the broad back window, he could spot a dog, leashed or unleashed, a quarter of a mile up Normandy, and he would tense his muscles and fix his gaze on that dog until he had passed by and out of view. Our neighbor across the street was teaching his big furry dog how to ride a bicycle. Almost every late afternoon the man could be seen riding up and down Normandy on the bicycle with the dog sitting behind him. This was a somewhat unusual sight, of course, which drew the attention of the neighborhood kids, of myself, and of Spit. In fact Spit was fascinated by it, although he preferred watching it from a branch in the oak tree.

My stepson Gibson visited from Nashville with his dog Jake. Jake was a felicitous enough dog, but Spit would have nothing to do with him. If Jake made congenial advances, Spit would bristle and climb onto the mantelpiece, or the refrigerator, or the rafters in the den. From there for long moments he would follow the dog's every move, no matter how mundane: eating, lying down, scratching at fleas. You will have to take me at my word that whenever Jake heard the theme music to the National Public Radio program "All Things Considered," he would immediately freeze, cock his ears, then proceed to dance madly about while he lifted his snout and howled to the top of his lungs, and this singular exertion would continue until the theme song finally ended. Gibson had warned us of this, and that it was the only piece of music to which Jake would respond at all, because Gibson said he had tried everything from Rachmaninoff to Elvis Presley on him, to be received by mere stolid indifference. Every afternoon we tuned to "All Things Considered" and watched Jake impetuously dance and howl, and none with more rapt regard than Spit himself, who from the rafters crouched low like a tiger and vigorously bobbed his head back and forth in rhythm with the dog and the music. I believe Spit was glad when that dog went on back to Tennessee.

Throughout our years together Spit would persist in interrupting my work, just as he had as a kitten in the Sun-N-Sand Motel. My wife the Cat Woman had induced me to start a book I had been postponing for years, a personal book about my days in New York. I had been putting this task off, and for sufficient reason: I knew it would be long and painful. She had set up a work area in the basement of the house at Northside and

66

Normandy, a cheerless, clandestine station that I came to call the Dungeon, and to which I forced myself to retreat alone five or six hours every livelong day for most of two years. She did not exactly lock me in, but it felt like it. How I suffered in that solitary redoubt!

Why, please edify me, was it that at other hours of the day when I called out to Spit McGee to come into the house and be with me, he largely disregarded me? But then I would be at my subterranean worktable with my pen and paper living out some distant, involved experience of the tumultuous 1960s, and who should suddenly jump up from nowhere onto the cluttered table but—you know who. I usually had the doors shut, but he had discerned on his own some surreptitious passageway for his ingress and egress that I myself, try as I did, was never able to locate, but that had to have led from the backyard on one end and the upper part of the house on the other. His entrances were so impromptu and my brain so far away on other years and more exotic locales that his precipitate leaps onto the table never failed to scare me badly. No amount of cajolery would induce him to leave until he was ready. As in the Sun-N-Sand as a little kitten, he would poke at my writing hand, then sit unbudgingly on my paper at exactly the spot where I was writing and stare right into my face. "What is the old fool up to now?" he seemed for all the world to be asking. "Please, Spit, I've got to make us a living," I would plead. Sometimes I even found myself promising him more strained turkey for infants. To no avail. He would have his visitations. After a time I would just sit there with him, and rub his neck and belly as he tenderly now gazed up at me. Then he would nuzzle me with his nose. "You're my boy," I would say to satiate him. When he started to doze off I would lift him and put him down the table a little way, and he would

67

remain there with me a long time until he eventually woke up and proceeded out of whatever imperatives to his secret tunnel outside.

He had his whole outdoor cosmos in our backyard, where I continued to watch him in the off hours in his sundry individual pursuits. There was something oddly primal about him, something consummately instinctual, which seemed to guide his movements, his concerns, his secrets. Cats live in a landscape of odors, I had read in one of the books, and he would glide along in the grass or among the weeds with his nose primed and ready, for what I was never sure. This whole area of the city was a nexus for innumerable pesky squirrels, and ever since he was an older kitten he had chased after them but had never succeeded in catching a single one, and for that matter has not to this day. With time his advances toward these little rodent vagrants have grown more and more fainthearted and perfunctory, and he and the squirrels seem to have established some implied truce of sorts, a kind of informal DMZ between them, and he will sit there and stare at them, and they at him, in querulous juxtaposition. Sometimes irate pairs of bluejays swooped down from the trees toward him, squawking at him in vociferous innuendo, and he and his mother, Rivers, would stand upright like kangaroos and hiss back at them, but nothing much ever came of this incipient territorial animus either. Across Normandy a little red-haired boy had a basketball goal in his driveway, where he dribbled the ball and shot baskets every day for a long time—the result of the boy's having attended a Meadowlark Lemon basketball clinic, the father had explained to me—and many was the time Spit would cross the street and sit on the edge of the driveway hypnotized by the boy and the ball, following every gesture with his concentrating gaze,

68

as if mulling what manner of animal is the human species. In his exterior universe Spit preferred moving nonchalantly in his quests and curiosities, because even then he had a somnolent aura about him, especially in the blazing Mississippi summers, but as I have earlier mentioned he could move very fast when he chose to. If it began to rain, for instance, and I opened the back door, he would dash into the house so swiftly that he was for the moment transformed into an oblong white blur.

We had a next-door neighbor on Northside named Hunter Cole who went by the nickname "Mack." Mack was a colleague of the Cat Woman's at the University Press of Mississippi, once a college teacher, and a photographer and writer with a percipient and tolerant eye. He became intimately attached to Spit, who traversed the bosky, overgrown terrain that separated our houses two or three times a day to visit him. I wished to get his unique perspective on Spit at that time, the year 1992.

In the mornings when Mack Cole opened his kitchen door and looked across toward our house, two white cats, Spit and Rivers, who appeared to him "like daisies on the brown landscape," would be picking their way through the leaves and underbrush. They claimed this grove, he gathered, for their morning toilet. This done, he remembered, they would pounce on small critters they had raked up. Then they began the long act of grooming themselves, and their energy doing this was to him a rousing spectacle. "They were finicky and individual," Mack recalled, "but still were like a team, or a troupe. Any watcher could spot what was singular about each of them and could appreciate it."

Rivers began secreting herself on the branch of a hedge on the far side of the back lawn, thinking, no doubt, she was well concealed. But even in the dark bushes she was so gleamingly white that anyone could see her. If Mack made eye contact with her, she returned a celestial and resentful look. From his very first visit, Spit caught our neighbor in his golden eye, Mack admitted, and was hard to resist. But for a time he scorned attention. Mack's stratagem was to sit on his heels with his back to him and then pat the ground with his hand. Spit would run up beside him as if it were his decision to participate. Mack was discovering, as I had, his weak side: curiosity. And I value Mack Cole's mini-portrait of Spit McGee:

I was mesmerized by his astonishing gold and blue eyes. I am told that some white cats have such eyes, but Spit's were the first and only ones like this that I've seen. When I took his picture, I regretted that the black-and-white film would not show the magnificence of those eyes. I recall that Spit was obedient for the picture-taking. Yet when I'd move toward him to focus, his curiosity would prevail and he'd spoil the sitting. He was compelled to brush his whiskers against the camera and sniff it out. In the heat of summer or the cold of winter, in dry spells or rain, he'd be bedded down in my backyard. I'd look out the window and see him asleep in all weathers. He looked like an ermine muff dropped on the pine straw. In the daylight hours, say, after ten A.M., anybody looking for Spit could be sure to find him balled up under the same tree. The nest of pine needles became Spit's daytime abode, but he took meals at his real home and for his nighttime rests bunked there too. At sunset he'd head out from my place at a rather sleepy gait. His winding route was the same every day. When he reached the wire fence at his home carport, he'd crouch for a count of five and then spring to the top of the post and drop lightly to the ground.

He seemed to float through his own special world.

JoAnne and I had difficulty in deciding whether to have Spit neutered. The consensus among cat experts was to do so when cats were little, but in my historical ignorance of cats I felt he should have one chance at least to become a father, although it was hard to believe he was approaching that age now. He would often wander the neighborhood and return dragging and dirty. I see now how wrong I was, as two imminent hazards to him will signally illustrate.

Once again, as he had as a kitten, he did not come home. But this time he was missing much longer. We searched everywhere. We wandered the vicinity tacking up flyers on telephone poles: *Young White Cat Missing. One Gold Eye, One Blue Eye. Answers to Name Spit McGee. Reward!* We took out classified ads and visited the city animal pound. As the hours passed, this time I knew he was gone forever, and I had only myself to blame for not getting him fixed. For a man who had once loathed cats, I was more miserable than ever. I kept the back door ajar at night and listened for every sound of Spit McGee.

Finally, on the fifth day, we went to the pound again, wandering about that sorrowful chamber where stray puppies and kittens looked out the wire cages with beseeching eyes to be granted happy homes by fortuitous human strangers. We went from one cage to another, drawn in the end to the final row. I walked up to a large pen of cats. There were four young cats inside. Three of them were awake and moving around. The fourth was asleep. He was white. As we stood there he opened his eyes. One eye was blue, the other gold.

I held him in my arms as we carried him away from Death Row. I felt the same churning emotions as I had

71

more than half a century before when I rescued my dog Skip from quicksand in the Delta woods. As we were signing papers at the checkout, the attendant said a man had caught Spit in a cat trap and brought him to the pound to get rid of him. When the attendant was not looking, I glanced down at a document on the desk and noted the address of the person who had ensnared poor Spit McGee and brought him in for euthanasia. The next day, I drove to that address. It was more than half a mile from our house. I considered paying a visit to that man. The Cat Woman was adamant. She had almost lost a cat, she said, and had no intention of losing a spouse in a cat trap, too.

And then, on the direct heels of Death Row, yet another disrupting thing happened. From the porch I was keeping half an eye on Spit, allowing him his backyard wanderings, but as dark descended, I lost sight of him. A man on a motorcycle roared down Normandy, swerved to the left, then disappeared around the corner. Later, after dinner, I called Spit, but he did not come. We looked and looked for him and finally saw his white tail poking out from under our bed. We found him crouched there, blood dripping from his back leg. He had apparently been hit by the reckless motorcycle driver. I made an emergency call to the animal clinic, and the benevolent Dr. Ray came to his office immediately and examined him. Spit looked up at me from the laboratory table; there was terrible pain in his eyes. The prognosis was a badly dislocated leg bone and internal damage. The doctor said he would be all right, but he had to have an operation that night. After that, he would be in a splint and bandage for ten days. Could he neuter him while he was at it? I asked. Yes, he could. "Then please 'fix' him," I said. "I'm too late already."

72

He came home a tripod, his back leg heavily bandaged. For three or four days I put him in my bed with me and nursed him, feeding him and giving him his medicine as I had done those weeks before when he was little in the Sun-N-Sand Motel. I would put the sheets over him just up to his neck, tuck him in, prop his head on pillows, draw him close to me, help him go to sleep. "Sleepy-time now, McGee," and he would look up at me with his drowsy eyes. Gradually he began to hobble around the house and to lie in the sunshine, always returning to me, settling in my lap as he recuperated. "No more trouble, Spit," I said. "Let's have a normal existence from now on." He would heed this counsel, and not suffer another mishap until years later when he had an altercation with an opossum.

CHAPTER 7

A Calico Waif

THE ETERNAL SOUTHERN SEASONS CAME AND WENT. The complicated mother cat Rivers continued to live rather much by her own solicitations and drifted about as she pleased. She was never gone for very long, and I was convinced of her ability to take care of herself against the external world. Spit McGee was relatively punctual, and although he spent long hours meandering outside, he seldom wandered beyond the next-door neighbors' houses and almost always returned before nightfall. Gradually I got him accustomed to riding with me in the car, and later in this story I intend to account a few of our more satisfying journeyings together. For now, however, I wish to postpone my description of these mutual dalliances to describe a serendipitous moment.

It was a cold November, unseasonable for these American parts. The branches in the trees in the yard were frozen solid, making crackling little echoes in the palpitant wind. All along Northside and Normandy were the sight and smell of spiraling wood smoke. My basement dungeon was frigid too, and I moved up into the dining room to work. Rivers and Spit were keeping themselves closely indoors, more often than not by the fire we had going all the time.

JoAnne was at a publishing conference in Atlanta. One late night in my bed I heard for a few seconds an unaccountable sound, a strange, muffled chirp that seemed to have come from deep underneath the house. Later that night I was awakened by it again. I took it to be a noise from the pipes, and I gave it no mind.

JoAnne returned the next day. Late that afternoon she heard the same small noise from under the house. "That's not pipes," she said. We went outside with a flashlight to the minuscule opening under the house, the same one through which we had retrieved the infant Spit McGee months before. The Cat Woman bent down and crawled on all fours into the darkness. I flashed the light into a corner. Caught there in the icy glow was a tiny solitary kitten, her eyes caught momentarily in the light, hunched up and shivering against the cold. She looked up at us with a pitiful expression of fright and panic. You could tell she had just about given up.

We took her inside. She was frosty to the touch. She could not have been more than three weeks or a month old. She was a calico. I had never seen one of those before. JoAnne sat with her by the fire and began rubbing her up and down to get her warm.

"Poor little thing," she said. "Let's keep her."

"Not on your life," I said, the misanthrope returning in an instant. I don't want any more cats. All they do is get run over or run away." I added: "And that's the ugliest cat I ever saw."

"She's not. She's beautiful. And she's hungry."

The Cat Woman took her into the kitchen, warmed up some milk, and put it in a bowl on the floor. She placed the pathetic creature next to the bowl, and the little cat immediately began lapping up the warm milk. She drank the milk for a long time, then glanced up expecting more. Who should stroll out from the bedroom in that moment but Spit McGee. When he sighted that kitten from several feet away his reaction was almost comic: he froze in his tracks and stared at the callow interloper in wide-eyed astonishment, touched with an uncharacteristic inhospitable expression. He gazed at her for the longest time, then turned around and went back into the bedroom.

How in heaven had this diminutive waif, starved, freezing, and nameless, ever gotten under our house? Where had she come from? Had she come on her own, or had somebody purposefully put her there? At least one thing was certain: she could not have lived much longer under the house in that impenetrable autumn tundra. "Poor little thing," the Cat Woman reiterated, and gave her some more milk, and then maternally held her in her arms in front of the fireplace again. The abandoned orphan began purring as she was rocked back and forth like a baby. That was when I began to suspect we were probably going to keep that cat after all.

The next day we had to drive to Greenville, Mississippi, far up in the Delta, for a meeting, and the Cat Woman insisted we take the kitten with us—given the circumstances of her unannounced arrival, she calculated, Rivers and Spit were likely not ready for a new intruder just yet. On the drive north the foundling was perfectly behaved. Most of the time she rested in the Cat Woman's lap, but she would also perch on the shelf behind the backseat and absorb the fleeting bucolic scenes: the stark flat land seared in glimmering layers of frost, the copious gray horizons, the plowed-under fields of cotton, the creeks and bayous with their floating shards of ice, the crowds of black people of all ages in front of the crossroads stores. Her decorum was in noticeable contrast to the deportment of Rivers Applewhite when she had driven me to distraction with her unnerving tantrums on the equally long trip to Oxford, Mississippi, not long after she had arrived that Christmas.

We left the kitten locked in the motel room with a bowl of milk and a DO NOT DISTURB sign on the door while we attended the meeting, and on our return she was nowhere to be found. Not another disappearing cat? We searched everywhere in that room without success, and asked the manager and all the maids if someone had mistakenly opened the door, allowing her to escape, but no one apparently had. We searched some more.

"Maybe she's curled up in the box springs," the Cat Woman said. I once had a cat who did that." So we lifted up the mattress, and then JoAnne crawled under the bed, and there indeed she was, wedged up in the bed springs fast asleep.

On the drive home the next day she explored every inch of the conveyance this time, then settled into JoAnne's lap and started purring all over. I began examining her calico spots, black, orange, and tan, interspersed with creamy white, which looked so perfectly contrived that even the most adamant disbeliever might have been seduced into seeing in their incredible symmetry the touch of a divine hand. Her longing luminescent eyes were the color of olive oil on the kitchen windowsill when the sun shines through. She looked over at me with these eyes and purred some more. And with that immaculate gesture she had won me over, as she likely knew she would all along.

I suggested then and there, about halfway between Belzoni and Midnight, that we name her Mamie Harper after my own grandmother.

"So we'll keep her, then?"

"But we'll have to check it out with Spit."

My grandmother Mamie Harper was to me one of the most beloved people ever to have lived. To name this kitten in this car on this day after her was a sort of amelioration, I suppose: a glandular buffer against the dangers, hazards, and toils I had so learned about that lurked out there for all feline creatures.

Rivers, as it turned out, would have nothing to do with the foster addition. She simply ignored her. As for Spit, Mamie won him over, although this required a few days. The kitten wanted to play with him not just part of the time but all of the time, and he was plainly not prepared for it. But then one day I looked out the window of the Dungeon and saw him in the yard in the now familiar tableau: teaching her how to sharpen her claws on the tree bark, how to climb trees, how to be sensitive to approaching dogs. A little after that, during another severe cold snap, I noticed the two of them together in the house, wrapped up in a furry ball on the bed. The next morning, with the thermometer on the back door showing eighteen degrees, Spit rousted me out of sleep at 8 A.M. by knocking all the things over in the bathroom and then led me directly toward the back door. I thought he wanted to be let out, but that was not it—he led me right to Mamie, who was waiting outside the closed door to get in. When the weather warmed up one afternoon that week, Spit went outside but immediately came back in, and I wondered too what that was about. He had returned to get Mamie, nudging her with his nose and then waiting for her at the door to come out with him.

78

As she started growing up, we began to call Mamie "the Cat Who Comes When You Whistle," and this was literally accurate. JoAnne, who said she had never known a cat to do this, discovered the proclivity quite by accident. An inveterate whistler, she was in the den whistling "Turkey in the Straw," or perhaps it was "The Blue Danube," and Mamie, who was in the kitchen eating, forthwith interrupted her supper and came straight to the whistler. We could even whistle while Mamie was on the far side of the house sound asleep, and she would immediately wake up and rush to the Cat Woman or me. Over the years people would ask, "How did you teach her that?" (If Mamie always came when you whistled, even the inaccessible Rivers Applewhite would come about 25 percent of the time when you wriggled your fingers, whereas if you did either of those with Spit, he would look at you as if you had lost your mind.) Mamie likewise acquired the habit of walking into the bathroom while I was taking a bath in the tub and sitting there and staring for endless moments at the water as if hypnotized, and then at me, moving her head inquisitively back and forth. I once asked our friend, the writer Elizabeth Spencer, who is another cat woman and proselytizing ailurophile, why she thought the young Mamie persisted in this bathroom ritual. "She wonders why you don't have your fur on," Elizabeth speculated.

It is funny how remembrance sifts and winnows a few tangible images for you of fellow creatures, supple images that memory itself is beseeching you to summon. With Mamie in these days it is my calling her name as she plays on the neighbor's lawn five houses away. It is along toward twilight of an effervescent summer's day, and the lightning bugs are out in driftless random, and the cicadas are buzzing in wild symphony everywhere, and Spit is at my side, and when Mamie hears me she lightly lifts her head in our direction and begins to bound toward us with the soft dexterity of a young doe, and gracefully leaps the fence in the most perfect of arcs, and on approaching us she jumps lovingly toward Spit and begins licking him on the nose. Mamie was a little lullaby.

At times she was like a giddy Delta belle—adroit, affectionate, flirtatious—at others sedate, pensive, withdrawn. She trusted us. One day I was sitting in the house when she entered the half-opened back door from outside and came up to me. She sat down in front of me and tenderly extended her right paw toward me. She was showing me she had injured it. There was a cut on it, and a piece of broken glass in her paw. Now that we had three cats, it was becoming increasingly difficult to load them all up and take them in for their shots. I had not long before found out about a young vet named Dr. Kirby, a recent graduate of the Mississippi State University School of Veterinary Medicine up in Starkville, who toured the city and countryside in his own mobile clinic making house calls with his bulldog, Bubba, always at his side. He looked sixteen years old, and his van was painted maroon and white in the colors of the Mississippi State Bulldogs, with the prominent likeness of a bulldog emblazoned on it, and he too will henceforth be part of this chronicle. I telephoned the ubiquitous Dr. Kirby, who was there in fifteen minutes with his on-wheels medical clinic and Bubba on the front seat next to him.

There was one disturbing retrospection. What if the Cat Woman had deferred her return home from Atlanta, Georgia, that time by another day or two? The old, wizened dog man could never have found the kitten under the house on his own.

80

When Mamie in her turn became pregnant, as with Rivers earlier, I could not help but feel a little sad again, because her poignant kitten days were over.

Spit had taken it upon himself to try to protect Mamie from the tomcats when they came in the mating period, and I would see him standing eye-to-eye and one-on-one with them in the nocturnal driveway. In these *mano y manos* he was valiant but outnumbered and, after all, was going up against the inexorable imperatives of Mother Nature her very self, so after a while he gave up and joined me every day in the Dungeon. With Dr. Kirby's reliable professional expertise at our disposal that a cat's gestation period is sixty-three days and the first-hand research I gathered by looking out the window, the birth of Mamie's litter could be plotted with some verisimilitude.

So in the eternal cycle she grew quieter, more reflective. Once I saw her lying on the carpet meticulously examining her growing nipples; she was no longer, at least for now, the giddy Delta belle. As the time gradually approached, we arranged a small box with a blanket on the bottom and put it in a closet, and who should immediately crawl in it and promptly go to sleep but Spit McGee.

She had four kittens. Overnight, it seemed, she looked matronly. Her eyes beamed with pride. There was something moving about the tiny orphan we had found under the house in the role of a mother. Motherhood! The timeless mosaic repeated itself. As Rivers had been with her kittens, Mamie was like a metronome. Every two and a half hours or so she would emerge from the box in the closet, where she had been nursing them and sleeping with them, and take a prolonged break to eat and relax, then she would go back again. Sometimes Spit would visit the closet and sit there looking at them. The normally aloof

Rivers Applewhite herself, who had been uncharacteristically solicitous of Mamie during her pregnancy, would go into the closet and rub Mamie's nose with hers. What is it, the sisterhood of God's maternal creatures at childbirth?

Ten days after the birth, the kittens' eyes had opened. Once when Mamie was taking her routine recess, I brought the box from the closet into the den and let the kittens crawl around on the carpet. When Mamie came back inside from the porch and saw what I had done, she was furious at me. It was the only time she ever hissed at me. Petulantly she took the kittens one by one in her teeth around the nape of their necks and returned them to the closet; for two days she would not have anything to do with me. From time to time when the mood was upon her she, as Rivers once had, would hide them in various crannies of the house. Sometimes we were unable to find where she had taken them, but Spit, who took enormous interest in these logistical matters, somehow always could.

The new arrivals were a diverse quartet. The largest of the males, a gray-striped longhair, we named George W. Harper after my great-grandfather—"Harper" for short. The orange longhaired male we called Bubba. The female tortoise longhair we named Bessie Graham, after the grandmother the Cat Woman had stolen from the loveless nursing home. The small black-and-white male was named Major after the Cat Woman's grandfather, but in time this would be lengthened to Major Major Major after the irascible character in *Catch-22*. The kittens were not yet a month old when we moved to a different house, a momentous odyssey for our brigade of seven cats, which I must now recount in some detail.

CHAPTER 8

An Old House by a Creek

CATS ARE TERRITORIAL BEINGS, MR. CLEVELAND AMORY and other inveterate ailurophiles had stressed for me in my earlier inquiries, perhaps more than any other animal species, creatures as they are of conservatism and routine, inquisitive but not especially adventurous. The place where they live is absolutely everything to them, its known contours and assumed familiarities. New places even as straightforward as motel rooms fill them with fear and uncertainty. Our seven cats were soon to enter beyond their will into uncharted terrain, and I felt for them.

The Cat Woman had been looking for a larger and older house for all of us. At first I paid her precious little mind, even as she conducted me through faubourgs like the historic Belhaven neighborhood, where I was born only a couple of blocks from Eudora Welty's house before my parents moved to Yazoo and where my grandparents and great-aunts lived years ago. She undertook this mission with a single-mindedness that would have shamed

Prince Metternich at the Congress of Vienna.

Then one day she chose an unaccustomed detour to work and fortuitously found *the* house, she said. She returned home with the news, glorious as a meadowlark, and forthwith took me to the place. It was indeed a splendid old dwelling in a serene and graceful vicinity, only a mile or so from the house on Northside, a substantial two-story with spacious rooms and gently sloping roofs and an acre of land dotted with towering white oaks and post oaks and elms and sweet gums and magnolias and old camellias and intricate, gossamer azaleas and secret little wooded enclosures and traversed at its downhill periphery by a sizeable meandering creek called Purple Crane. The place had a patina of continuity. I can only confess in my heart, especially after my many previous years in what might only be called "bachelor pads," that it was the house I wanted all my life, but I was hesitant to tell her right then.

"I have a feeling we're going to buy this house," she said.

"What are we going to buy it with?"

"Why don't you write a book about your dog Skip?"

The Cat Woman knew, of course, how to get to an embattled writing man. But not far from my considerations, I hasten now to admit, was Spit McGee himself: What would Spit think of this strange house—how would it fit into his own honest regional autonomies? And the nervous and eccentric Rivers Applewhite? And another not inconsiderable matter was that Mamie Harper's four kittens were only three weeks old. How to manage such a definitive journey with a solicitous young cat mother and her vulnerable offspring?

While the bankers were laboring on mortgage and other matters, one late afternoon of false spring on my insistence we took Spit over to the new domicile. He sniffed out every last corner. He climbed the unaccustomed stairs and stalked all the closets and rooms. On the broad lawns outside he slinked everywhere in a junglelike crouch right out of "The Short Happy Life of Francis Macomber." He went down to Purple Crane Creek and sat there for a long time looking at the water. Then he climbed a white oak and surveyed the encompassing vistas. When he finally came down I could tell he was baffled.

I have mentioned Spit's bizarre psychic facilities and shall persist in doing so in this story when I know he is right. He knew something was going on, and he did not for one moment like it. He began spending more and more time with me on my worktable in the Dungeon. Chaos soon descended. As the furniture movers began coming in the house on Northside, the calico young mother Mamie was hiding the kittens everywhere. Rivers stationed herself on the rafters in the den and glowered down at the bustling intruders. When Mamie presumed to come out from her hidden kittens she too bristled at the Cat Woman and me.

It was wisely concluded to wait until everything was moved out to transport the cats to the new home. On the last night in the Northside house with only a few items of furniture remaining to be transported, Mamie and the kittens drowsed unsuspectingly in a box in front of the fireplace. Spit looked up at me knowingly from precisely the spot in the dining room where I had delivered him at birth. "*Live, kid, live!*" We were departing a place of many felicitous moments, but of sad ones too: where Spit had been hit by the motorcyclist, where his three young siblings had died of anemia, where we had found the starving waif in the bitter cold.

The next day we used a cat cage to convey the seven of

them to the new establishment.

The house had been built in 1940 by the son of a man who had been governor of Mississippi twice and had not been elected either time, and for this he had made Ripley's *Believe It or Not*, for as lieutenant-governor in both 1927 and 1943 he had succeeded on the deaths of the presiding governors. His was the only family to live in the house before us. Every Christmas afternoon of my faraway childhood I drove out in this direction, the "new section" of town then, with my grandparents in their vintage Dodge to look at the Yuletide decorations. As we traveled down the Old Canton Road, could I have mystically divined then that a mere hundred yards or so away down a side street was the very house in which many years later I would dwell with a beautiful wife and seven cats, including a big white one with one blue eye and one gold? Was it waiting there for me all along?

The adult cats traversed their different surroundings with abject trepidation, as if risks and surprises awaited them beyond every corner, only in time to be assuaged by their in-born curiosity. They even went on a brief hunger strike. By the movements of their ears I could tell they were assessing by day and by night every solitary sound from inside and outside. Mamie was now bedded down with the kittens in JoAnne's closet, and Spit himself vanished under a bed upstairs until we found he was protesting that we had forgotten to bring his litter box from the other house. (Although he rarely used it at the other house, it somehow made him feel at home.) It took a while for them to grow accustomed to the old furniture in new places, to bigger fireplaces and taller ceilings, to the Cat Woman's mother's ancient Singer sewing machine and my own mother's turn-of-the-century Steinway baby grand, both brought out from storage. I was disturbed about the neighbor's dog, which came into our yard the first night. The cats gazed incessantly at alien walls and chandeliers, and walked up and down the stairs several times a day to get used to them, and it took Mamie a couple of weeks to permit the kittens to crawl around on the floors. When Rivers and Spit began exploring the big backyard in earnest and when Mamie finally started allowing the kittens outside, I knew they were getting acclimated.

I have always been obsessed with the classic paradoxes of time, of time *warps*, of mystical visitations into the distant past—no single book by anybody ever affected me more acutely in this regard than H. G. Wells's *The Time Machine*, which transported me back and forth in time's specific locales so graphically that it made me quite deranged—and this brand-new vicinity beguiled me with fancies of the human beings who had dwelled here years earlier, along this very creek, on this very property, within this very neighborhood, their lost voices, their transient joys and hopes and fears, and this surely had to have been heightened for me because of the simple actuality of ownership.

As I sat in the backyard watching the cats establish their hegemony, I tried in my imagination to conjure what this particular swath of the Lord's earth was like two hundred years before, let us arbitrarily say. So I again went down to the Eudora Welty Public Library, which I had previously drawn upon for my random investigations into cats, and even to the state archives, to derive some tangible notion of what might have been transpiring on this exact ground in A.D. 1800 and beyond. My precise property, and my cats', was only about four miles from the old Natchez Trace, the historic Indian trail and then stagecoach roadway from Natchez to Nashville, the great artery to the

Old Southwest with its pioneers and explorers and entrepreneurs and notorious highwaymen. So this backyard had not been all that remote from bustling and egregious human activity.

It was then a neighborhood of dense hardwood forests through which the Choctaw Indians could roam and hunt freely. Our surrounding area was soon bought by white settlers at $1.25 an acre. Later in the century our site was very near Grant and Sherman's Union lines in the Battle of Jackson, during which Sherman burned down most of the town. Out of the mists of history, then, one might surmise that the view from my present workroom, and the one afforded my cats from their perspective in the trees, were Choctaw Indians, isolated farmers, and Yankee soldiers. And a survey of our exact property taken in A.D. 1821 amazingly indicated the same giant post oak trees that still flourish here. The place did indeed have continuity, although I have no solid documentary evidence that any of the long-departed human souls who traversed this soil actually themselves had cats.

The four kittens would be Mamie's only litter. Three of them had Maine coon cat ancestry with long, multicolored hair, patches of white under their chins, and big bushy tails. Bubba was orange and white. Harper was gray, white, and black and looked like a raccoon. Bessie was a tortoise. Major Major Major was a shorthair with a taut, muscular body like that of an Olympic gymnast; he was similar to Mamie and Rivers in physique. They were beautiful and fun and we could not bring ourselves to give any of them away until they were over six months old. The longhairs were interesting to look at, curled up together or flipping their impressive tails at the squirrels and bluejays. Major Major Major was the climber in the group and spent most of his time outdoors skittering up to the tops of trees.

I was taken by the sight of Spit and the four kittens in the backyard. While Rivers and Mamie posed with self-absorption on a fence or sat on the back steps half watching, Spit would perennially stand guard to see that they did not wander into the street. He would "herd" them like a sheepdog to keep them from straying too far. I was impressed by this avuncular vein in him. As with Rivers when Spit was these kittens' age, and he with the young Mamie, he began teaching them how to sharpen their claws on the bark of trees, and later how to climb trees for their own protection. He was also instructing them on how to climb *down* a tree—a more arduous task than climbing up, I saw—meticulously swaying backward as his claws attached themselves to the bark. He did this time and again, and after diligently watching him they began to follow his example.

So for a while we had the seven cats—Rivers, Spit, Mamie, and the four kittens. Then David Rae and Susanne spent a month with us before moving into a house in New Orleans. They had their two cats, Modie and Sunny, with them, who were segregated in an upstairs room. That was nine cats in all, and when Dr. Kirby came to give all of them their shots he said it reminded him of the zoo.

When the kittens got bigger, we finally gave Bubba, the orange male, to a cat-loving friend Jane who lived nearby, and Major Major Major, the white-and-black male, to Claudette, great-granddaughter of the governor whose son had built the house we had just moved into. Both of them, I am glad to report, would have healthy and happy homes. (Not until three months later, however, did Claudette ascertain that Major Major Major was, in fact, a female.) That left us with Harper and Bessie, so that we were down now to a menagerie of a mere five cats. And that, too, would soon be qualified.

We were approaching another emotional intersection. Keeping the two kittens, and with Spit and Mamie very much with us, became too much for Rivers Applewhite. Ever since the birth of Mamie's litter, with the exception of a brief period in which she acted kindly to the new mother and infant kittens, Rivers before our eyes grew increasingly disenchanted. Try as we did to curry her with attention, she became more and more withdrawn and dissatisfied, as if she did not choose to share any of her own life with the others. She more or less ignored them all. Spit himself, who got along well with other creatures as much as just about anybody, became irritated with his mother's regal aloofness and began ignoring her in turn, an oedipal estrangement if ever there was one. Rivers was gone for longer intervals, her visits back to the house less and less frequent. Then she stopped returning at all. After a few days we discovered she had moved in permanently with another family three houses up the street. The family did not know her name and adoringly called her Snowflake. They owned no cats and had a swimming pool in the backyard, around which Rivers, they told us, lounged contentedly much of every day. Whenever the family went out of town, I went up to feed her. "I'm glad you're happy, Rivers," I said to her. Not too long after that, however, she left these generous souls and moved in permanently with yet another hospitable family, it was discovered, half a mile away. Since she was a Highway 51 cat, I suppose, she always had to be on the move. So the little kitten who had come out from under the Christmas tree with a red ribbon around her neck back then, the one whose most fateful destiny was to become the mother of

Spit McGee, was finally gone from us. That left us with four.

As he grew up, Harper would encompass me with his warm and gregarious temperament. He was totally lovable. He had huge brown eyes and an affectionate gaze that he bestowed in democratic élan on friend and stranger. Harper may have been the sweetest creature I have ever known and he sought the Cat Woman and me out to be his constant companions both in the house and outside it. He remained exceptionally close to his mother, Mamie, to whom he demonstrated his faith unabashedly. He was also a funny little individual with fluttering ears and a shaky bushy gray and white tail, and I think he desired us to know that he was happy and cared for us.

"This one is my favorite," visitors would often say. He was predisposed to spending long hours sleeping with me, nestled loyally in the crook of my legs, and he and Spit became close companions, surveying together the verdant corners and wooded cul-de-sacs of their neighborhood suzerainty. Among my vivid recollections are seeing Spit and Harper lovingly together in our yard.

Harper's sister Bessie was skittish as she matured, reluctant to join in spirit, but soon grew to be a fine and sociable young cat. She followed JoAnne everywhere and at night preferred to sleep curled around Spit, whom she obviously adored almost as much as she did the Cat Woman. Of all the cats in our life she was the most dexterous huntress. Four days in succession one summer she brought mice in the house, and she also brought me dead lizards with such frequency that I nicknamed her Lizard Borden. Always, at the first approach of winter, she began to sprout her winter coat, so dense and prolific that JoAnne called it her "Neiman Marcus fur," and even if it was seventy-six degrees of a meteorologically schizophrenic

December fortnight, she would prance about the outdoors unbothered by her heavy winter apparel. And as with the Nashville dog Jake, who waltzed and howled whenever he heard the "All Things Considered" theme music, you will have to take me on solemn oath that when she was lying on the floor or the sofa, whenever Elvis Presley was singing on the stereo, she would swish her tail in precise rhythmic beat to the song, and only to Elvis, I am swearing to you.

Their backyard environs were much larger now, and I was always watching them from my upstairs workroom as they familiarized themselves with it. It was strange not having Rivers out there perched in a tree following the movements of the others. When Spit went down the back steps outside, he would tarry for long moments on the patio, looking all around—up into the trees, down along the undulating lawn. What's going on out here today? he seemed to be pondering. Their daily life on the new ground was always an adventure. The young ones, Harper and Bessie, at first followed Mamie wherever she went, then took to trailing behind Spit, emulating the way he climbed trees and his light tiptoes as he investigated things.

A solitary hawk in a white oak tree at sunsets riveted Spit's attention. In the ersatz spring of February his nemeses were the swarms of screeching blackbirds who descended by the hundreds from the trees onto the lawn. Spit gave them their independence for a while, but soon learned that if he suddenly ran toward them they would brainlessly take off in their skyward clusters and head elsewhere, and Harper and Bessie learned this too. Living across our creek in a big white house with columns was former governor William Winter, one of the great

Southern governors, who had a hyperactive little schnauzer named Fritz. While the governor raked his own leaves, or mowed his grass, or sat on his front porch reading a book, Fritz traipsed his front lawn barking boisterously at the recent interloper cats, demanding their attention. Spit, Mamie, Harper, and Bessie sat on their knees in a tight cadre and stared back at him for moments on end until they concluded to disregard him pretty much forever.

As winter passed into spring, Spit grew more and more drawn to Purple Crane Creek, a tributary to be reckoned with. On normal days it was serene and meandering enough, but it overflowed in the torrential rains and took on a life of its own then, less a creek than a river with its cascading water and its rushing cargo of branches and leaves and desultory debris. Cats do not like water very much, and in such moments the four of our cats would sit together in a row under the canopy on the back steps with the rain making its grand noises on the roof and silently gaze out at the transformed Purple Crane.

In a matchless early spring as the dogwoods reached bloom and the foliage deepened and the very atmosphere itself grew heavy with its cachet of rich, perfumed Mississippi scents, and the cicadas commenced their mindless cacophony, and the diaphanous mists arched from the dew-wet grass, the Cat Woman and I sat at dusk in the backyard watching our cats in their multifarious occupations. Harper had become as athletic as his mentor Spit, and the two of them engaged in pursuits and retreats that bore resemblance to human footraces, wild wrestlings, competitive climbs high into the oaks and sweet gums and elms.

It was along about then that we became aware of an obstinate seasonal presence, a veteran citizen of the creek, we would learn: a bullfrog who with the coming of the spring began, regular as time itself, his deep, resonant croakings in the twilight and long into the dark, dusk after livelong dusk into the summer and early fall, when he would inexorably recede once more into wherever bullfrogs go in winter, and then return again into the Aprils as before. He became integral for us to the changing seasons and to the mellowing landscapes. When we first heard the croakings of that bullfrog, the cats stood there and listened, their ears twitching in response, and then went down to the creek to see what this might be. It was Spit, of course, who eventually tracked the stranger down. I saw him at the edge of the creek that spring, looking at something in the water, his long white tail moving back and forth in his usual keen inquisitiveness, as it always did when something interested Spit McGee. I went down there myself to investigate. I knelt next to Spit and followed his inestimable gaze. There, partially hidden beneath a little green lily pad, was the bullfrog himself, eyes ebony dark in the fading light, who though smaller bore in the instant a certain benign resemblance to the mystical Yoda in *The Empire Strikes Back*. I believe Spit was proud of his discovery, and over our years together, whenever the frog returned in his eternal, recurring echo, would seek him out time and again down at the creek as he had that first long-ago evening, and sit there for lengthy moments just looking down at him, a white cat and an old, eternal bullfrog there together at Purple Crane.

A year or more went by. Thomas, who worked at Lemuria Bookstore up the street, had become our cat-sitter whenever we had to go away. One night we returned after two weeks on business in Los Angeles, and Thomas

94

reported that our cat Harper had been acting strangely. He had been squabbling with his sister Bessie. All four cats were in the house when we arrived from L.A., and Harper pushed at the back door with his paws demanding to be let out. I opened the door for him. It was the last time I ever saw him.

I remembered Harper would often follow us when we went out for a long walk in the neighborhood. We would have to take him back and lock him in the house. He was the only one of all the cats who ever did this. Did he just walk off with someone?

I choose not to dwell at length on the disappearance of the sweet, affectionate Harper: telephone calls, classified ads, flyers on telephone poles with the promise of rewards, visitations to the animal pound. I did a taped interview regarding the book I had just published about my New York days on the National Public Radio program "Fresh Air," during which the host allowed me to announce in considerable detail the disappearance of our little cat Harper and to provide for a national constituency a detailed description of him, right down to the name tag and telephone number on his collar. I felt certain he would return. We posted wanted notices at the animal shelters and received one call from a lady who thought she had found him—we went over but it was not Harper. He had always seemed happy and adjusted and had never once been gone overnight. But he never came back.

I observed the heart-wrenching sight of Spit, sitting for long hours on the back steps looking out into the distance. I knew he was waiting for Harper to come home. "He's gone, Spit," I said. He, too, finally gave up. That was four years ago. I wonder if he remembers Harper now. To this day I constantly think of Harper, and if he is alive: if he is happy and warm, or hungry and cold.

95

In my sadness I read a poem by Thomas Gray that someone had recommended to me. It evoked the kindly and gentle Harper for me. It was called "Ode on the Death of a Favorite Cat," and was written after the poet's cat fell into a goldfish pond and drowned. The last quatrain went:

> *From hence, ye beauties, undeceived,*
> *Know, one false step is neer retrieved,*
> *And be with caution bold.*
> *Not all that tempts your wandering eyes*
> *And heedless hearts is lawful prize;*
> *Nor all that glisters gold.*

CHAPTER 9

"How Can You Have a Cat?"

And so there were three: Mamie, Bessie, and, of course, Spit. They are the ones still with us today. And I pray for a very long time to come.

A year went by, then some of another. I finished the book on my boyhood dog Skip, the one the Cat Woman had suggested I do to help pay for our house. In truth, I would have written that book anyway: it was something that needed doing, as I should have known all along. But here, reader, is a confession: in all the sad things I had written about in books before, I had never once in the actual writing shed tears. Writing the last lines about the death of Old Skip, I found myself crying. The Cat Woman, of course, noticed this when I came downstairs and gave her the last page. She gently dabbed at my face with a handkerchief:

Walking alone in the teasing rain, I remembered our days together on this earth. The dog of your boyhood teaches you a great deal about friendship, and love, and death: Old Skip was my brother.

They had buried him under our elm tree, they said yet this was not totally true. For he really lay buried in my heart.

I spent a long time outside with Spit McGee that day. He lay sleepily in my lap as we sat in the dappled sunshine under the dogwood by the creek and watched the unexpected sight of a pair of exquisite young ducklings floating past. "Where did they come from, Spitty? Where are they going?"

Mr. Loomis, my editor and publisher in New York City, who had grown up as a boy in Ohio with an honored little dog named Meo and still talked about him, wished me to undergo a three-week national book tour on *My Dog Skip*. "Just emphasize how special Skip was," this dog man counseled me. "Don't disclose to anyone that you now have cats." He included with this a letter from his resourceful young son, Bobby Miles, who had recently sunk twenty-four out of twenty-five free throws in a competitive basketball shootout in Sag Harbor, Long Island, and also had just gotten a distinguished dog named Nellie, several full-color photographs of whom Bobby Miles enclosed for me, although he himself, unlike his father, charitably chose not to chastise me against talking about my cats on my travels. The Cat Woman was to accompany me on this ambitious tour, and I was reluctant to leave Spit, Mamie, and Bessie for such an extended interval, but we furnished our cat-sitter, Thomas, with sixty-four cans of cat food and thirty-two jars of Gerber strained turkey and were on our way.

This tour included signings at various bookstores

around the country. At the request of book buyers I found myself signing books for dogs, hundreds of dogs, both living and deceased.

"Please sign this to Cindy."
"I'll be glad to, Cindy."
"I'm not Cindy. Cindy's my cocker spaniel."

"Sign this to King Solomon."
"Are *you* the King Solomon I've read about?"
"King Solomon's my golden retriever."

"Will you sign this to Leopard?"
"Is Leopard here tonight?"
"Leopard's in dog heaven. Just sign it to him. To the memory of Leopard, please."

And on and on: to dogs, or to the memory of departed dogs, named Spot, Tolstoy, Lady, Bonaparte, Sadie, Eddie, Betty, Teddy, Shaquille O'Neal, Knute Rockne, Mary Ann Mobley, Oprah, White Toes, Cassandra, Don Imus, Ginger, Oedipus Rex, Lou Holtz, Chester, Renaldo, Charlie Chaplin, Queenie, Truman Capote, Pinto, Stripes, and yes, more than a few Skips. A number of bookstore owners announced that patrons bringing their own dogs would receive discounts, and this worked agreeably in most places, with dogs of all breeds and nonbreeds in attendance (including English smooth-haired fox terriers who were the living image of Old Skip himself), with one notable exception: at an establishment called Square Books in Oxford, Mississippi, a serious dogfight erupted, with six or eight dogs going at it in a most terrific and spirited manner, and a sleepy-eyed Saint Bernard trying to escape this fray knocked me out of my chair asprawl onto the floor. It was at another Oxford event that the majority leader of the United States Senate, Mr. Trent Lott, approached me and declared, "Skip had to have been a Republican, didn't he?" "No, Senator," I replied. "Skip was a Jeffersonian Democrat." And at a later occasion at Shakespeare and Company on Madison Avenue, the Cat Woman and I were judges in a contest to select the two dogs there who bore the closest resemblance to American writers, the prizes going to a cocker spaniel that looked like Eudora Welty and a great Dane that reminded us of Kurt Vonnegut, Jr.

In these distant, disparate travels I confess I sometime failed to follow my editor's admonition, and some American people found it hard to believe that I now had cats rather than dogs; in that regard the ancient dog-cat animus seemed still very much in flourish. "You mean you wrote about a dog and now have a cat?" When I told them about Spit McGee they sometimes became hostile: "How can you have a cat?" I could have told them how much I missed Spit down in Jackson, Mississippi, and that I had already telephoned him three or four times, getting Thomas to put the receiver to his ear. "Spitty, be a good boy. I'll be back soon."

I returned home to a tremendous influx of correspondence in which countless strangers all over the nation had enclosed photographs of their dogs. One person in Connecticut sent me a picture of his Dalmatian named Tyrone and told me Tyrone could do something Skip probably could never do, and that was eat artichokes properly.

I still have an enormous cardboard box filled to capacity with these photographs and challenges. As was his habit, Spit sat on my worktable and inquisitively sniffed at the contents of these diverse missives, rubbing his whiskers on the faded photos of excellent dogs dead now a quarter of a century or more. A most unlikely sight we must have made, an all-white cat with two different-colored eyes and a disheveled author in a big upstairs room looking over this unusual plethora of items. "Let's pay a visit to Skip's grave, McGee," I said.

CHAPTER 10

PRIVATE JOURNEYINGS WITH SPIT

I ALWAYS WONDER WHAT SPIT IS THINKING—HOW HE sees things, what he remembers, how he deals with reminders, what is in his soul. I talk to him a lot. Often in fine weather we sit together down by the creek and I tell him things, such as what I am trying to write, or what I am doing tomorrow. He sits there mindfully enough as if trying to understand. He is not always a good listener, of course, and gets whimsical and proceeds with his own concerns whatever they may be, but there are times and moods when he seems to listen very closely to me. "It's tough being a human sometimes, Spitter. What's it like being a cat?" Unlike Edwin M. Yoder, Jr.'s royal cat, Pharaoh, whose owner as you may recall claimed him to be lineally descended from King Mongkut of Siam's court cats, Spit could only claim a simple pedigree of the heart. There was no way to discount his rare and incredible intelligence. It was not just this intelligence itself, it was the manner in which he expressed it—his absorbing eyes,

102

actions, nuances, the way he would sometimes penetratingly look at me as I talked to him. Whenever, for instance, he saw me with a packed suitcase, as per the description of my friend Ben of his cat, Bill, he knew I was going away for a while and this always made him angry; he was curt with me and paid no farewells. When I returned from a trip he was usually not at home but then reappeared very soon. Still indignant, he would proceed to ignore me for a certain period of time. He also constantly knew when I was trying to trick him—to come inside the house, for example. He would sit on the back patio examining me closely, flipping his questioning tail: What does he want now?

There is a Jill Krementz book of photographs of writers at their desks. One of them is of Spit and me in my large cluttered workroom upstairs. He had been badgering me as usual on my table and then decided enough of that and was resting on the carpet behind my chair when Ms. Krementz's shutter clicked, as if he had given up on me and wanted to be alone but did not wish to leave the room itself, so that he could still be there with me. As time passed we were together more and more in that workroom.

One day we encountered a mutual peril. He was half asleep on my worktable when suddenly from outside the back windows came a prodigious cracking sound like an explosion, a sound of utmost danger. He and I both jerked up. I could hardly believe it. An enormous tree was in the act of falling and was heading precisely in our direction, descending maddeningly toward the very roof of our room. On instinct and nothing more, I shoved my chair away and leapt onto the floor as far away from the windows as I could manage. Spit swiftly followed, and we hit the floor simultaneously, he landing wildly on my back and clinging protectively to me. In that moment there was a powerful, rending crash that sundered the entire room. We lay sprawled there together for the longest moment. Then I looked up. Great sturdy branches of the tree and a large part of the trunk had splintered through the roof only a few feet from the table. He and I glanced at each other and then finally got up. If that tree had been twenty feet longer the reader would not have this book about Spit McGee before him now. It was a close call. It turned out to have been a prodigious delinquent hackberry tree in the side yard, a singular species of tree noted for its febrile root system, which cataclysmically split out of its own roots and rained down on us of its own mindless accord. It took three weeks to repair the roof and the room, but fortunately for us neither Spit nor I was struck by even a solitary splinter.

I have dealt before with Spit's intuitive capacity. Not for a moment do I wish to exaggerate this facet I sometimes discerned in him, but there were occasional moments when I did not know how otherwise to explain his responses to certain situations. Foremost for me in this regard was his behavior one particular afternoon in our backyard. Not long before there had been a horrible mass shooting on the grounds of the high school in the town of Pearl, Mississippi, about twenty miles from Jackson. A sole deranged boy had first murdered his mother at home, then with cold adolescent cunning opened fire with powerful rifles and shotguns on his classmates, killing two of them and wounding several others. The youngsters in the school had been traumatized. Bullets had fallen all around them and they had witnessed firsthand the bloody murder and maiming of their friends. This proved to be the first in an appalling succession of similar massacres in schools around America. An English teacher at the Pearl school had written to see if she could bring her ninth-graders, the youngest students in that school, to our house for a visit. The young students had been reading the children's book I had once written and had even toured the vestiges of that story in my old hometown. A trip to our house to talk about such things would be good for the youngsters after the tragedy they had survived, the teacher said.

They sat on the grass in the backyard with RC Colas and Moon Pies as we talked about books and the writing of them. There was a melancholy look in their eyes at first. Spit was out there among them—and I can only testify he must have perceived something in the atmosphere itself. I know I am right on this: never once the hail-fellow-well-met, never facilely gregarious in large crowds, he nonetheless mingled tenderly with those children, wagging his tail at them like a dog, falling on his back and extending all four paws in the air to exhibit his idiosyncratic resting posture, climbing trees, running around in circles, allowing them to examine his different-colored eyes, consuming a few Moon Pie crumbs offered him, then sitting alertly in the midst of them as the discussion turned to himself. What does Spit eat? they asked. I brought out a container of Gerber strained turkey to demonstrate his reaction to the shrill metallic sound of the top as I opened it. How does he get along with the other cats? What does he think of dogs? How much does he sleep? Where is his mother? Has he ever been injured? Spit continued to sit there with uncharacteristic solemnity now as the talk of him ranged round and round. They finally said good-bye to him one by one, individually petting him about the head and ears, and he even accompanied them to the school bus as they were departing. For me it was among his proudest hours, and I told him so.

He likewise remained protective of Mamie and Bessie, much as he had when they were kittens. They followed him under the house in case danger ever came. He even scolded Bessie whenever she tried to push her mother away from the cat food platter. He demonstrated to them how to lie on top of the heating duct under the oven in the kitchen on cold days when there was no fire in the fireplace.

I thought it a little sad that Rivers Applewhite was now out of our lives and never even deigned to drop by for a visit anymore. Rivers had, after all, been the blood progenitor. Testy though she always was, she had for a long time been a part of us. The three of them did not seem to miss her at all. They did things their own way. Inside the house they played what could only be described as hide-and-seek together, the younger cats Mamie and Bessie going about hiding under chairs and sofas and beds while Spit searched for them, stalking them on African jungle toes and always flushing them out. They did things together. In an unexpected snow flurry one day the three of them stood in a small shifting circle outside, leaping upward in unison and biting at the unfamiliar snowflakes. Sometimes at night all three of them slept on top of the Cat Woman as she lay on the sofa.

Bessie with her orange face, pink ears, white paws, and furry gray coat persisted in being with the Cat Woman everywhere, following her all over the house, sitting on the kitchen counter and watching her as she scrambled eggs, trailing her in the yard when she watered the plants, an uncanny symbiotic relationship. She looked at JoAnne all the time as worshipfully as she might some rare and beatific saint. I called it her Joan of Arc stare. When the Cat Woman was away from the house, Bessie would go

106

looking for her everywhere. If I was sitting in a chair, she would jump into my lap and look joylessly at me: *Where is she? How do I find her?* In my entire existence on this earth I have never witnessed one living creature adore another so much.

I have just described Spit's response to the young kids from the school in Pearl. Yet by far the most straightforwardly psychic of the cats, in two aspects at least, was the calico Mamie Harper. This is a region of tornados, and the radio and television stations are responsible about reporting tornado alerts. Almost invariably, long minutes before an alert is announced, Mamie will start acting crazily—stomping with her paws, running around erratically, hiding under furniture. (I had always heard about cats acting similarly before earthquakes.) Then there was the matter of Dr. Kirby, the peregrinating vet. He would arrive at the house in his medical van at every appointed date that the cats' various inoculations expired. The first time he did so there was no problem with Spit and Bessie, who allowed him without protest to take them one by one out to his van to administer their shots. The problem was always Mamie. She somehow knew the vet was there before he so much as rang the doorbell, and forthwith would find an impossible hiding place. We set a day the following week for him to try again to do Mamie, making sure she was securely in the house just before he came. The same thing happened. Indeed, a quarter of an hour or so before the actual appointment she simply disappeared again. There had to have been something downright organic in her composition about such things. How else to explain it? I have no notion whatever of how she could have predicted the vet's arrivals in this way. Finally we had to resort to putting her in a cat cage shortly before the next appointment; her wails of protest could have been heard two blocks away. But this time it worked, and Dr. Kirby took her in the cage to his van and succeeded with the shots. After that, for days and weeks whenever Mamie was outside and sighted the mail van, or the Federal Express van parking in front of the house or merely moving down the street, she bolted away and found herself another hiding place somewhere.

I will not go so far as to say that our three cats acted telepathically when it came to the phenomenon of television, which JoAnne and I sometimes watched in the evenings, but they sometimes reacted in distinctive ways when it came to certain images on the screen. One night we were watching Hitchcock's *The Birds* and the three cats were solidified by it, staring silently from in front of the screen, and when those maniacal birds came out of the trees with their loud screechings to attack terrified human beings, the three of them, led by Spit, went right up to the screen and bristled in a trio tandem. The most striking response to TV was that of the Maine coon cat Bessie. We were watching a documentary on the sinking of the Titanic, and when the water started impetuously rushing into the ballrooms and bars and the captain's nest itself she looked up at the screen, then proceeded to hide her entire head under the rug near which she had been lying.

Then there was the circumstance of Spit McGee and televised ball games. Ever since he was little Spit had often sat with me watching ball games, and at first it always disturbed him when I would suddenly rise and yell inanely at something or other that had transpired, a referee's blasphemous call, perhaps, or some spectacular play, especially during Ole Miss Rebels or Texas Longhorns or New Orleans Saints football games, and Spit would get up and stretch himself self-consciously and retreat into the kitchen as if embarrassed by my behavior. But after a time he grew accustomed to these unseemly outbursts and more or less took them for granted, merely looking up at me as he did when he thrust his paws on my writing hand at my worktable and seeming to ask, "What's the old fool upset about now?" I believe he came to enjoy being around me during these games, sensing as he might that they were of more peremptory import than the inchoate political talk shows, and in the unfolding of time we watched many a significant sporting event together. Although I will not go so far as to suggest that he himself might have been consciously watching the action on the TV, he certainly seemed contented enough sitting there with me on those many days. By way of historical substance, for instance, and merely to illustrate that Spit and I have lived together through consequential moments of many sorts, he was with several companions and me in our den when we watched Mark McGwire going after his sixty-second home run and we were all debating whether this would be the night he broke the Roger Maris record. I have a large portrait of Babe Ruth on the wall, and the Babe seemed there with us in aura. Spit was sitting next to me on the sofa, and when in his second at-bat Big Mac hit one down the left field line and into the bleachers and everyone jumped up and shouted, *"He did it! He did it!"* Spit was so caught up in the celebrative frenzy that he straightened up on the sofa and performed one of his phenomenal high-arched leaps, which landed him on all four paws in front of the fireplace.

Some time before this I concluded, if you can believe it, to get him a leash. Knowing him in his heart as I believe I did by now, I was sure he would not like this at all, but perhaps he could at least come to terms with it. I was forthwith in this decision because I felt the time had arrived for the two of us to do some traveling around together. In truth, something inside me as I grew older was compelling me to take Spit McGee to some of the meaningful landmarks of my own past. To the most confirmed of ailurophile readers I request that you not specifically ask me why and do not press me unduly on this: it was just one of those compulsions of the heart, and if it seems rather self-serving, then so be it. Spit McGee was my cat, and time was, after all, passing, and I was reaching a point in my life when I felt I needed Spit with me in these indwelling places as a matter of mutual support if nothing else.

I bought a cat leash at the pet store. It was the best you could find, they assured me, and completely safe. Spit McGee, they said, could never break away from it and get hopelessly lost in unfamiliar surroundings. That afternoon I approached Spit, who was reclining on the picnic table in the backyard, and casually as could be attached the clasp of the leash to the ring on his collar. I wanted us to practice. "Come on, boy!" I said, and persuaded him to jump off the table to the ground. Then I began leading him around.

Have you ever seen those old B Hollywood Westerns in which some auspicious rider of the range tries to break in a wild mustang without so much as the embellishment of a saddle, and how the intrepid mustang keeps throwing the cowboy onto his rear on the hard sagebrush earth? Well, this was an equivalent. The expression Spit gave me as I tried to lead him around in that backyard was one of abrupt and seething betrayal. His eyes blazed with hot resentment. The leash itself was only about five or six feet long, as I recall, and he circled back toward me and began biting the cuffs of my trousers, then holding on tight to

110

them and pulling angrily at me. He was trying to pull *me* around. When I resisted and began trying to lead him again, once more he circled back toward me and tried to trip me onto the ground with his feet. Pitiless is what he was. As I wavered, he moved back a foot or so, then rammed his whole body into my knees from behind. Yes, I did say *rammed*. In American football this would plainly have been a fifteen-yard-penalty for clipping and an automatic first down, or as the new and more sterile terminology had it, "blocking from behind," and I stumbled over him and fell bodily into the grass. The leash slipped from my hand and he arrogantly leapt onto the picnic table and glared down at me again. Do any of you think a cat cannot laugh? He was laughing at me! Now there was the unmistakable sound of real human laughter. The Cat Woman, who had been watching from the kitchen door with Mamie and Bessie, was laughing as she seldom had since those long-ago days when I was trying to teach Spit to retrieve sticks at the old house. "It's not going to work!" she declared.

I retreated into the kitchen and brought out a container of Gerber strained turkey, a saucer, and a spoon. As casually as before, I snapped the leash onto his collar and lifted him off the table down onto the ground again. Again I tried to guide him with the leash. This time he sat adamantly on his haunches and refused to budge one single inch. I put some strained turkey in the saucer and placed it before him. Given his relish for this favorite delicacy I could not believe what he did next. With the meretricious right paw he was always jabbing at me with, he pushed that turkey away as stubbornly as if it were a fortnight's leftover corn gruel.

That is when I gave up. When a man has one woman and three cats making fun of him on his own hard-earned

111

land, he had better have efficacious alternatives. I went back to the pet store and told the proprietor of my problem with my cat and the leash. He counseled that I get a somewhat longer leash, about ten or eleven feet long, say, which would give any highly independent cat more freedom of movement, he said, and also a feeling of implicit trust. He could make me one. He had one ready in two days, a handsome enough item with a sturdy yet flexible plastic cord. It was not inexpensive either.

I went outside again and attached the new apparatus to Spit's collar as he lounged in the grass. Then I crawled craftily on all fours about ten feet away, giving me two feet or so leeway in slack on the leash, and quietly as could be sat down. I had brought a paperback book with me and when Spit roused himself, which was soon, I pretended to be reading. I always was distrustful of Spit when he merely cocked one eye at me, especially the golden one. He rose, yawned, glanced over at me, stretched himself, then started ambling indolently down toward Purple Crane Creek. I tossed away the book and, leash firmly in hand, crept in the direction he was headed. He reached the creek. I believe he was looking for the old bullfrog. When he stopped, I stopped too. He turned his head and saw me on my knees on the grass. He stared suspiciously at me for a long time, then noticed the slack leash string on the ground. He sniffed at it, then pawed it. When he started walking around again, I got up and followed him at a discreet distance, never once tugging at the leash. We had been together very long years, and had arrived at various modi vivendi in that period, and I hoped this was one of them. But I was unsure.

I really believe he knew what I was up to. Did he want to humor me this time? He did not seem to mind the longer leash, especially since I was not pulling at it. I rehearsed this with him for half an hour or so in the backyard as he moved about on his missions and was gratified to see the arrangement was working, at least tentatively so.

Now I had to accustom him to riding in the car. He had never liked the car too much. Once David Rae had tried to take a humorous photograph of him with his paws on the steering wheel of the car parked in our driveway to appear as if he were actually driving a vehicle as Old Skip used to do, and he had, of course, balked at this. But now as I challenged him he was more inquisitive than he had ever been about the inside of the car and began perusing the front and back seats, the dashboard, the floors. Maybe he would not be as unprincipled as I had feared about driving around, especially since almost all his earlier car trips had been to the veterinary clinic before we discovered Dr. Kirby. And on this I was not very wrong. On a pair of trial runs he was peevish at first, but then blissfully succumbed to what our neighbor Mack Cole had perceived long before as his main weakness: curiosity. The fleeting exterior scenes as we drove along, the places and people, seemed to amuse him. He grew relaxed. He was trusting me.

That was the genesis of our journeyings together. As I have previously admitted, I had always been obsessed with old and supple places from my own past and was perpetually returning to them out of remembrance and belonging, a maddening writer's sustenance in such matters, I suppose, and I would return alone to these places time and again and suffuse myself with their lingering secrets. But now I believed Spit would be a satisfying companion, and since we had been sharing a life for a long time anyway, it was worth the try. I needed my cat.

113

I began with a swing around Jackson itself. My own private aspect of Jackson existed in another time, when it was nothing if not a somnolent state capital town, lethargic in those wartime summers, and poignantly rooted. These were my childhood years, when I came down from Yazoo City to spend a good part of each summer with my grandparents and great-aunts. In our long walks around town everything, people, places, seemed of a piece: impalpable and connected. "Setting out in his world," Eudora Welty wrote of *her* Jackson, "a child feels so indelible. He only comes to find out later that it's all the others along his way who are making themselves indelible to him." Once Spit found his favored station in the back window behind the seat of the car, yielding him a view of the universe outside, I found myself chattering away to him about these venerable matters. This was much better than talking to myself, as I sometimes did on these mystical excursions, and—who knows?—he might have been listening a little. At any rate, my soliloquies did not seem to be bothering him. I parked the car on North Jefferson and clamped the leash to his collar. We got out and commenced walking along the same route my grandfather Percy, dead these nearly fifty years, and I once had on our way every late summer afternoon to the Class B Jackson Senators' baseball games in their derelict little wooden green stadium down at the state fairgrounds. The familiar blocks seemed unchanged with time, and as Spit strolled ahead of me the full length of the leash, I felt the spirit of my grandfather. Jabbering away to my cat, I lectured him on how important grandparents are.

Next we drove to the state capitol building, where I had spent so much time meandering about as a child. On this day Spit and I had it all to ourselves as we walked the magnificent marble floors of its interior, with the bell of the majestic rotunda above, and his ears moved to the rich descending echoes of it. One day we drove out to my familial village of Raymond, twenty miles or so from Jackson, and paused at the antebellum house my great-grandparents had built in the 1850s. The present owners indulged us freedom of these grounds, with Spit on his farthermost leash. He walked up onto the front gallery, which had once run red with blood, where my great-grandmother had nursed the wounded of both sides after the Battle of Raymond, and in the house itself he followed me into the bedroom where my grandmother and all her sixteen siblings had been born, and my mother too. We went into town to the red-brick structure that had quartered the newspaper offices of my great-grandfather George W. Harper, after whom the beloved furry cat Harper who had run away those months before was named, and to the exact spot where the town well had once been, and into which Sherman's federal troops had deposited Major Harper's printing presses. At the ancient graveyard not far from here, a few feet from the old family plot enclosed in its rusty wrought-iron fence, Spit and I sat on the grass and had a picnic, a ham sandwich for me and Gerber turkey for him. In moments such as these I had never seen him so companionable and well behaved, and in sedate places like this cemetery I allowed him off his leash and watched him as he walked down to the deeply shaded plot of the Confederate dead and promptly began taking a nap on the grave of a poor lad from Tennessee.

I took him one day to Yazoo, forty miles to the north. Every house, every street corner, every *tree* held memories for me, and I began chattering away to Spit again about all this as we cruised the immemorial town, and I was glad to have him with me on this day as he sat on the dashboard;

his presence itself was more than enough. It was a sly and silent town back then, and we kids had absorbed its every rhythm and heartbeat. It was abundant with alleys behind the paved thoroughfares inherited from an earlier day, little pathways running with scant design or reason behind the houses and stores and chicken yards and barns. They are here to this day half a century later, and I stopped the car, got Spit on his leash, and we wandered for a long time along the very same alleys.

Next I parked the car at my old school building and the two of us began walking the six blocks along the boulevard called Grand Avenue to the house of my boyhood. Spit and I walked by Rivers Applewhite's house on the corner by the bayou, then the house where we had left oatmeal cookies we had made with a mixture of castor oil, dill pickle juice, milk of magnesia, and worm medicine for dogs in a gift-wrapped package inside the front door for the Baptist Ladies' weekly meeting and hid in the shrubbery and watched as the ladies spit out the vile stuff.

Now we were at my house, etched there against time. I know every inch of this house; my sweetest dreams and deepest nightmares are filled with it. The present owners, whoever they are, were not there, and the two of us roamed the front and back yards. I lifted Spit up to a window and allowed him a glimpse of what had once been my room. There were no college pennants on the walls of it, no battered oak desk, no Corona portable typewriter. Farther on, the parlor seemed bereft without my mother's baby grand. My father's easy chair and his big shortwave radio were gone from the side room, filled now with alien furniture. Then at the back of the house to the place where Old Skip lay buried, near a small grove of shrubs not far from where my basketball goal had been. The earth around the goal was always bare from our strenuous footfalls, hard and compact and useful, but now the yard was neat and manicured. Did no boys live in this house? I pointed out Skip's resting place to Spit. How could I have expected him to be reverential? He walked up to the familiar old elm tree, much taller now, of course, in the branches of which Skip and I had had our tree house, and began to sharpen his claws on the bark, then climbed it and stationed himself just about where the tree house had been and looked down at me as I paid my deferences to Skip.

I had planned this trip to my hometown on this afternoon in particular because it was the exact centennial anniversary of my father's birth. I had brought a couple of roses with me and we drove up toward the cemetery, a lovely bucolic expanse that I knew about as well as any place on earth. First I showed Spit the witch's grave, out of which that fiendish hag had escaped in 1904 to burn down the entire town, and he scented with his nose and whiskers the broken chain links surrounding it. Then I led him by the leash to the splendid towering magnolia behind which I had hidden myself to play my mournful echo to "Taps" for the funerals of the Korean dead. And then to the spookiest vicinity of the old section of the graveyard, where Skip and I on a bet with my sadistic chums had spent an entire dreadful summer's night in a war surplus pup tent with the lightning bugs and the tossing shadows and the ominous rustlings all around. Spit had never seen tombstones before and he wandered about poking his nose on a few of them, then leapt onto the most forbidding one of all, the mossy gray crypt of the Gilruths, among the oldest and most honored denizens of the town.

I got him in the car again and we drove up to the "new section," as we always called it. In 1948, my freshman year

117

in high school, the old section in which we had just been wandering had for all purposes reached its capacity. It was in that year that the new section was opened on vast adjoining hills separated from the old by an emphatic little valley, the geological divide between the two precise and recognizable. After all the years the new section itself was running out of room. From its original perimeters to the farthest crest out at a verdant horizon of sweet gums, oaks, and cedars, these once untenanted hills were now crowded to filling with the tombstones of the vanished generation I once knew. They were now opening an even newer section in some rises and descents to the south.

I unhooked Spit's leash and let him roam. It was a day of ponderous purplish clouds and acerbic winds springing down from Memphis and the Delta, and I was bundled well against the chill, but Spit jumped onto one of the most prominent tombstones and let the north wind ruffle his white fur. I was drawn to the sight of him wandering circuitously among the stones bearing the surnames of all those people I once knew.

I was standing now at the grave of my father, one hundred years old this day. I thought I should say something ceremonial, but it was not unlike the time he lay dying in the King's Daughters Hospital down in town and I wanted to tell him that if I ever had a son I would name him after him, but I could not say it. I put one of the roses on my mother's grave next to him, and then the other on his. "Thank you, Daddy" was all I said. At that moment Spit returned to me from his graveyard investigations. He stood there by me. What would my father have thought? He deplored cats as much as I ever for the moment had. But, I thought in the instant, he might have liked this one.

Spit was very much a Christmas cat. Perhaps this had something to do with the fact that his future mother, Rivers Applewhite, had come out from under a Christmas tree those years ago in the house on Northside. With the acquisition of the leash, Spit went with us this past year to the fine old farm out in the country where you cut your own Christmas tree. In previous years our tree had been loblolly pines or blue cedars, but this time in Spit's company we picked a big, ceiling-high Virginia pine.

We always had family and friends on Christmas Day, and Spit was particularly attracted to the collective exchange of gifts; he always got gift-wrapped Gerber strained turkeys. I had a sister-in-law named Sara who now lived in Atlanta but before that in Muscle Shoals, Alabama, where she had a radio disc jockey show called "Sara of the Shoals." She was an animal-lover, so much so that she even had a high regard for spiders. A spider once wove a beautiful web over the front door to Sara's house. I saw that spider. She was quite elegant, I must concede, with long slender legs and bright markings on her back, and her web served a dual purpose, Sara said, to catch food and lay her egg sacks. Sara called the spider Charlotte, of course, from *Charlotte's Web*. The spider was very sociable and actually greeted visitors at the door by crawling to the bottom of the web. She was there for four or five months, and then one day simply disappeared, almost as our Harper did.

Sara was always drawn to Spit as much as young Bailey Browne was. "Christmas in Dixie is a joyous time," she once wrote me, and allow me to record her words here as another neutral perspective of Spit, "especially with Spit McGee. There he is on every Christmas Eve, on his back in front of the fireplace with his paws stretched in the air, visions of Gerber baby food dancing in his head. I'll

119

always remember how on Christmas Day he sits in the middle of all of us on a throne of wrapping paper. This is what Christmas is all about, he reveals to me through his odd-eyed gaze—family and friends, Leontyne Price on the stereo. Spit is the perfect host, a fine Southern gentleman if ever there was one."

This past Christmas, in similar ambience to our foray into Yazoo and to our later ones, I got Spit on his leash and took him to another unforgettable venue from my distant past, the site of my grandparents' house on North Jefferson in Jackson, three miles or so from our present house, where every Christmas morning of my childhood and boyhood I drove with my mother and father from Yazoo. Every year they would be there on the gallery under the magnolia tree imperishably waiting for us, the four of them—my grandparents Mamie and Percy and my great-aunts Maggie and Susie. Then at eleven in the morning, never later, we would sit at the ancient table that had been my great-great-grandmother's for Mamie's ineffable holiday feast, and I would look around me every year at each of them, as if all this were designed for me alone. Then, after the rattling of dishes, we would settle in the parlor again, drowsy and fulfilled. Finally my grandmother Mamie, standing before us by the fire, would gaze about the room and always say, her tone at once poignant and bemused: "Oh, well, another Christmas come and gone."

I was glad once again I brought Spit with me on this Christmas Day. The house was no longer there, long since a parking lot for the Jitney Jungle across the street. The magnolia next to where the gallery had been was dying, its gnarled branches seeming to reach upward in feeble supplication toward the skies. Spit and I got out of the car and I led him around the grim asphalt, cold and wet now from the early morning Yuletide rain. Spit paused at the woebegone magnolia to scratch his claws on its bark, then followed me, investigating the spot where the front porch had been, and where at this very moment years ago the four of them would be greeting us now.

Spit was now sitting next to me where the dining room had been. "Let's go on home now, Spit," I said. "They're waiting for us."

The Hollywood people had begun filming *My Dog Skip*, using the settled town of Canton, sixteen or so miles north of Jackson, which had faithfully preserved its historic edifices, as the surrogate for Yazoo. The filming itself would prove to be a reunion of emotion and remembrance for me, and I concluded as I had with Raymond and Yazoo to take Spit there with me, to observe something of the activity and contrivance. Three or four times that torridly hot summer JoAnne and I gathered up Spit and his leash and drove there, and these visits even more than the ones to the present-day Yazoo afforded me an appropriate opportunity to project Spit back to my 1940s.

Hollywood was zealously using all the faithful appurtenances of the World War II era, right down to the Studebakers and Hudsons and DeSotos with the gas ration stickers on every windshield, the vintage traffic lights, the period dress, the wartime food ration booklets, the old copies of *Life* and *Look* and *The Saturday Evening Post*, the baggy woolen baseball uniforms, the boxlike Philco radios, the Victory Garden in the backyard of the house representing mine with its scarecrow replica of Hitler, the one that Skip was always attacking. Watching the actors depicting my long-departed blood kin and my dog and my childhood chums, not to mention me *myself*, was a déjà vu of the most impressive kind. As for Spit himself, he wandered these time-imbued sets with a sense of purpose, I felt, which had to have derived from the same persistent inquisitiveness that was his forte, and he became a welcomed presence among the nomadic grips and gaffers and carps descended there with their logo T-shirts testifying to their work on movies all over the globe, not to mention the extras and stand-ins and actors and actresses and, yes, the *dogs* themselves.

One day the Cat Woman, Spit, and I were following a scene from a distance and I was attracted to several figures sitting together in some rickety baseball bleachers. There were the movie actor Kevin Bacon, playing my father; the actress Diane Lane, playing my mother; the little actress playing Skip's and my adored Rivers Applewhite; and, yes, the Jack Russell terrier playing Skip himself. They had *eight* dogs playing Skip, because Hollywood can apply makeup to dogs just as they can to people—puppy Skips, adult Skips, old Skips—including the dog named Moose, who starred in a popular national TV series of the day called *Frasier*. But the principal Skip in most of the scenes was Moose's son, whose name was Enzo. One afternoon, out of what must have been the most percipient of canine recognitions, Enzo, whom I had not yet been introduced to, sighted me sitting in a chair behind the camera. He looked up at me momentarily, then jumped onto my lap and began licking me on the face and nose. None of this was lost on Spit McGee. The Cat Woman had him on the leash not far away, and he forthwith led her straight up to Enzo and me. The dog was still in my lap as Spit propped his paws on my legs and stared straight at the dog, who stared right back, and that was it for Spit's first encounter with Enzo.

Later Spit met Willie, Rivers Applewhite, and even the child actor playing the character Spit McGee. Someone took a photograph of this latter meeting, and a local newspaper ran it over the caption: SPIT MCGEE MEETS SPIT MCGEE. Spit's most fulfilling moment, I believe, was when he saw young Bailey Browne, the aforementioned dedicatee of this story, who was a child extra in many scenes. As was the real Skip with the real Rivers Applewhite, Spit was a regular fool about Bailey Browne. Bailey had recently given me a handsome ceramic plate on which she had painted in her own hand:

WILLIE MO
and
BAILEY B.
FRIENDS FOREVER
with
SPIT McGEE

When Spit saw her in her plaid 1940s dress, he walked right up to her and nudged her with his nose. Bailey embraced him and said, "Spit, this is the funnest thing I ever did."

At the conclusion of one of these filming days, Spit had a more prolonged session with the dog Enzo, who was carousing on the grass with the three puppies playing the one-month-old Skip, the two-month-old, and the four-month-old. The dog trainer was nearby, and picked up Enzo and brought him over to Spit. I have often specified Spit's incipient distrust of dogs, but this was a small dog, and I watched as they sniffed each other out, then started cavorting agreeably together on the lawn, tussling around the way kittens and small puppies do: Skip and Spit, a 1940s tableau and a song in the heart, I can tell you. And when the three little puppies walked over, Enzo and Spit cavorted with them too.

If you do not count our confrontation with the killer hackberry tree, Spit had not faced any tangible hazards in an exceedingly long time, ever since he had been struck down by the motorcycle at the house on Northside. But he was fated to face another one now.

One afternoon not long ago I noticed a puffy area near the back of his neck. It had to have signified a wound of some kind. I telephoned Dr. Kirby. He faithfully arrived in his mobile clinic and examined him. Spit had been bitten by something with very sharp teeth, he declared. "A dog?" I asked. "No, sharper teeth. Maybe another cat." The doctor took Spit to his main office overnight to shave the hair around the injury and disinfect it and to give him penicillin shots.

Spit returned the next day with a bald place on his neck and marks on his skin. The doctor left some pills. He was all right, he said, but be on the lookout for strange stray cats.

One early evening a week or so later I looked out the back door onto the lawn and saw an incredible sight. I could not believe it. Spit was standing nose to nose with a possum!

I have no idea how many of my more urban readers have ever seen a possum, or for that matter if you have any notion of what a possum is. He is ugly, that's what he is, and sinister-looking. In the North they are called opossums, but down here out of nothing but rank opprobrium we expurgate the *o*. They are renowned here, and villainous. Where had this possum come from? How on earth had he arrived in our backyard? Had he come down from somewhere faraway on Purple Crane Creek? In my astonishment I initially could do nothing but absorb that uncommon spectacle of Spit standing straight up to the possum. The grotesque beast had a pointy white

124

face, sharp, fanglike teeth, sharp-clawed toes, round black ears, round furry posterior, and a naked tail half as long at least as his body itself. He looked *prehensile*, and as he stood there challenging Spit on Spit's native soil, he was making a sound that I can only describe as *Ch! Ch! Ch! Ch!* I knew possums were rodents, like very big rats, and that they were nocturnal creatures who ate almost anything. Perhaps this one had come up from the creek to purloin some of the dry cat food we usually left outside for our cats. Surely it was this repulsive invader who had bitten Spit.

I reached for the most convenient weapon, which was a broom, and rushed out into the yard. I approached the possum—he was actually larger than Spit—and began swiping at him with the broom. He looked up at me with his beady eyes and at first refused to budge. Then he began negotiating a gradual tactical retreat. *Ch! Ch! Ch! Ch!* Spit followed along behind me as I shoved the broom handle at the elusive brute. In little time he disappeared beyond the oak trees into the dense undergrowth across the street.

"You're a brave boy, McGee," I said. I swooped up both the platter of cat food and Spit himself and carried them into the house. Spit immediately leapt to a window and looked outside. There was no sign now of the possum. I soon discovered, however, another puffed-up area on Spit, this time on his lower back near his tail. Once again Dr. Kirby answered my summons. It was a similar wound as before, and again he was going to take Spit with him overnight.

"The possum did it," I said.

"The *possum*?"

I told the vet what I had seen, Spit in the backyard challenging that uninvited savage. "Possums aren't to be trifled with," the doctor warned. "I'd try to get him myself but I don't have any possum traps." He advised me to keep Spit and the other cats safely inside and to contact the animal control people first thing the next morning and demand them to come and set out traps. That night I phoned our neighbors, including Governor Winter across Purple Crane Creek. None of them had seen Spit's adversary. The next morning I phoned the animal control office, but they were out of traps too. This time I got a shovel and began meticulously searching the entire backyard and beyond. Spit again trailed behind me. He knew what we were looking for. I went across the street into a secluded, wooded area. I was about to give up when suddenly I saw an object protruding from inside a hollow tree: a long hairless tail straight out of the Age of the Dinosaur. I started banging at the tree with the shovel. Two little girls on bicycles happened by and tarried to observe the sight of an adult man swinging away at a hollow tree with a shovel. As with the kids who once watched me throwing sticks for Spit, the girls were laughing at me. They stopped laughing, however, when the misbegotten beast suddenly emerged from the tree. I took another swing at him and got him on his rear. He started loping across the street toward Governor Winter's house, vanishing in a clump of trees and shrubbery.

For several nights we would not let the cats outside. We never saw the possum again. But I retain the memory of the undaunted Spit McGee standing up to that carnivorous marsupial bully in protection of our principality. I suppose if you stretch it a little you could count it the fifth time I had saved his life.

Spit sleeps with me more than ever these days. I sleep a lot and have horrendous dreams: of being hopelessly lost in

126

unnatural gloomy outbacks; of wandering discom-
bobulated and without funds in desolate stretches of New
York City and no way to get back to my beloved Cat
Woman and cats in Mississippi; of entering lugubrious
chambers filled only with people I once knew, now long
dead; of dashing through faraway airports trying to make
flights home and the contents of my suitcase spill out all
over the floor; and on and on of being alone and lost in
heartless, forbidding places. I frequently have bad dreams
about Spit's welfare. These nightmares of Spit remind me
of ones I had of Skip years ago as a boy, and as a grown
man of Pete: inestimable dangers to them, losing them
forever on revolting and treacherous terrains.

I have these evil dreams of Spit and sometimes when I
wake up I write them down, such as this one: "3:15 A.M./
1/19/97. Here's a dream I just had. Spit and I are in some
scary foggy place. I am carrying him in my arms. We are at
the foot of a hill. I feel the beating of his heart. We are near a
rambling house with a big back porch. There is a party going
on and all the people there are people I once knew who are
dead. Spit jumps out of my arms and starts running away. I
run after him but he vanishes over a hill and is gone forever."
And: "4:00 A.M./3/12/97. Spit and I are on a spy plane over
Russia. The dream tells me we were American spies. A
strange cat, called 'the Purple Avenger,' very skinny and
vicious, teeth like needles, long claws who works for the
Russians tries to attack Spit. 'Nyet!' I say, and chase him
away. Now Spit begins to run away. He hopelessly disappears
over another hill. I never see him again. 'Come back, Spit!'
But he doesn't come back."

When I awaken from these awful images, I feel Spit
sleeping on a pillow next to me. I wake him from his sleep
and he looks at me with his drowsy blue and gold eyes. He
gathers closer to me.

CHAPTER 11

THE GENERATIONS

ALLOW ME TO BE LOGISTICAL FOR JUST A LITTLE WHILE. What do our cats do all day? How do they structure our own daily lives? I am presenting this specific catalog not only because I believe it might interest various of my ailurophiles, but to illustrate how far I may have progressed as a student of cat behavior. And, beyond that, what have I really learned as a human being from my cats?

In the first place, they do not do a lick of work. They may *think* they do, but they do not.

Spit McGee's habitual conduct, as you may by now have perceived, can sometimes be as intricate as a minuet. It all rests on his moods, which are many. He stays outdoors almost all of every day when the weather is sunny, and always in the morning, except for his forays inside for a meal or to check up on me, which he often does. He always comes in at night. In the hundred-degree weather he invariably sleeps in the yard or on the driveway lying on his back with his feet up in the air. When it is

128

cold, and Mississippi does have stringently cold winter days, he still naps in the sun on the picnic table in the backyard. He often goes down to the creek for a decent interval to investigate what might be transpiring there. Then he begins making his rounds of the neighborhood, ambling across the streets in front of and to the side of our house and into the neighbors' yards. What is he looking for? People? Other cats? What does he find? What does he do? There is only one other cat in the vicinity, and the dogs around here are all kept inside or behind fences. Whatever, his daily missions seem organized and finely tuned. When it is raining he is inside all the time, "knocked out" as I have earlier described it, as quiescent as any zombie.

Mamie also stays out a good part of every day. Our next-door neighbor Ann reports that she has several preferred secret spots in her yard, from which she silently absorbs the passing scenes, never getting in anybody's way.

Bessie hardly ever goes outside unless you put her out, and then she seldom stays there very long. She prefers to be near the Cat Woman all day. She is by far the most vocal of the three and seeks attention mainly by meowing. She has an incredibly extensive vocabulary of sounds and a most impressive delivery of them. She will look you right in your face and tell you when she is hungry and there is no food out or if she wants dry food rather than canned or that her litter box needs to be cleaned or that her mother, Mamie, is at the back door waiting to be let in. Her language is much too intricate to explain in this little section, as if I understood it myself, but she is a garrulous and filibustering talker if ever there was one. Sometimes she reminds me of a monkey, for monkeys, I have been advised, can often carry on three or four conversations at once just to get attention. If there is a more vocal cat

129

talker in Western Christendom I would appreciate knowing who it is.

Cats are animals of habit and these habits shape our own hourly existence whether we want them to or not. Spit is the most persistent of the three in all matters, which must be an expression of his tenacious IQ. Unlike myself, he is a pernicious early riser. He often sleeps close to me, but sometime between 4:30 and 6:00 A.M. he initiates his purposeful cycle of cajoling someone into letting him outside.

He no longer knocks over things in the bathroom to get you up; his ruses in this regard have become more direct and individual. Since he knows I could sleep through an artillery barrage, he long ago gave up on me, so he concentrates completely on the Cat Woman. First he puts a paw, with no claw protruding, on her face. If that does not work and she covers her face with the sheet, he puts his paw on her hair and tousles it all over. He then proceeds with this least subtle of harassments by extending his paw more and more into her head until she finally gets up and lets him out. Occasionally she can trick him into a few more minutes' sleep by holding him tightly next to her in the crook of her body and sedulously scratching his head until he himself goes back to sleep. This tactic is usually ineffective, however, and he resumes his systematic pawing. On really sleepy mornings the Cat Woman sometimes lifts him up and puts him outside the bedroom door and slams it shut. But this merely buys her a few more minutes at best because Spit will work on that damned door until he finally, with the bullishness of a Green Bay Packers offensive tackle, pounds his way back into our room and jumps right onto the Cat Woman's face. If this likewise fails to succeed he emits a loud, low, mournful meow, something he does only in the worst of

130

extremities and that is always highly disruptive because it is so uncommon. When the Cat Woman hears that fateful demand, she knows he means business and she has the good sense to respond. She has no idea what he might try next, she confesses, and is too intimidated at this point to wait and see. When she at last gets up, Spit waits at the top of the stairs outside the bedroom until he sees she has reached the bottom stair before he comes bounding down. He waits to make sure that she is not trying to dupe him again.

If he wants our attention when we are up and around, he jumps onto a nearby table or counter so he is on our level. If you are walking through the kitchen, he gets on the counter and waits for you to come by and, much as a traffic cop might do, thrusts out his paw to stop you. If you are sitting down and he wants to be petted, he leaps onto the table nearby and gets you to look right in his eyes. He puts a claw into your hand, gently at first, and if there is no response, then harder and harder until you lift it away and pay attention to him. He has always had a remarkable sense of where I am. Although he is most likely outside pursuing his multifarious assignments, his inner clock obviously tells him when I am finally awake and functioning, and he will come in and leap onto the dining room table while I read the mail and affectionately visit me there. He considers these important visits, during which he rubs his nose on mine and looks into my eyes with the sweetest and most docile of demeanors. And later in the day, of course, he will enter my workroom upstairs and try to disrupt my writing until he finally tires of this. Sometimes he will climb to the highest shelf of a bookcase and sit there for minutes on end just looking down at me. At others he will go sound asleep on my table or on the carpet next to my chair. For some reason neither Mamie nor Bessie ever comes into my workroom.

How do the cats signal to get outside? If Spit wants the back door opened he will jab at you with his zealous right paw. Bessie stands straight up, props her paws on the door, and waits. Mamie scratches on the side of the cabinet that holds our cookbooks. As for getting back inside, Bessie jumps up on the back door and hangs by her claws, her childlike orange face barely visible through the glass at the top of the door, while Mamie patiently sits at the back steps waiting for someone to happen by and open it. If someone does not appear soon, Bessie considers it her responsibility to search out JoAnne or me and take us to the back door to let Mamie in. I have no idea how she knows that her mother is there. Spit usually scratches audibly on the door. But at night if we are having a dinner party or company over and Spit wants in, he leaps onto the window ledge outside whatever room the guests are gathered in and gazes demandingly at us through the glass. One dark blustery Halloween night not long ago, for instance, with evil, pulsating bolts of lightning all around, several of us were having dinner by candlelight around the dining room table. There were a couple of children in our number and we were telling them ghost stories. Someone began reading to them Poe's "The Black Cat." At a particularly ominous juncture in the narrative Spit suddenly jumped onto the windowsill outside and pressed his fat face on the glass, an agitated white silhouette outlined against the encompassing autumnal dark, and this accompanied by another diabolic flash of lightning. The children shrieked in unison, and I will confess I almost did too.

Spit, Mamie, and Bessie have highly distinct and evolved personalities, and these emerge most obviously when there are guests or workmen in the house. Mamie

132

with her deep blood antennae always senses someone outside the family approaching; even as with Dr. Kirby, she not so much sees or hears him, and long before he reaches the front door she is gone. She refuses to deal with anyone new. Bessie, however, craves new people and insists on being in the middle of any gathering. When a visitor arrives she greets him effusively. If the plumber is under the kitchen sink, she will be there too, and she follows the pest control man everywhere, likely because of her expertise with bugs. Spit usually makes his appearance after everyone is settled in and engaged. That is when he appears at the window demanding to be let in. He makes what I can only call a histrionic entrance, then strolls through the room and checks out each person individually. If the people are to his liking, he takes a seat in the center of everything. If he wants to be petted, he intuitively jumps into the lap of the one person most likely to be persuaded. Sometimes he merely sits on the floor and appears to be assiduously studying the entire group. Then, in time, he will flop over on his back, thrust his legs up high, and take a nap.

Mamie almost always sleeps with us at the bottom of the bed. Bessie seldom comes upstairs at all and never sleeps with us. Spit changes his nighttime bed with his many whims—one month on the sofa, the next in our bed, the next in the guest bed.

These inexplicable rituals go on and on. Denizens of habit as they are, cats can form new ones at a moment's notice. As an example, rearranging the furniture in the living room to put up our latest Christmas tree inspired Spit for weeks on end to change his favorite lounging spot from the rug in front of the fireplace in the den to a newly placed chair in the living room. Mamie will eat only on a dish placed on the kitchen counter, and before she dares to eat she initially looks around to make sure Spit and Bessie are not near at hand. Bessie only eats from a dish in the laundry room. Spit, I can assure you, will eat anywhere. Many a conversation with the Cat Woman revolves around surveying and analyzing the cats' new habitudes. I suppose I had come a long way. Larry King or Geraldo Rivera or Ted Koppel of our contemporary era seldom entertain such absorbing and enigmatic topics, not even Monica or O.J. among the disparate cast of our relentless and frenetic American day.

Carpenters were building a new addition onto our house. They were there every day from eight to five for more than five months. Spit began hanging out with them, watching with astute regard all aspects of their work, the more intricate and robust the better. They had with them every day an amiable young chocolate Lab named Chelsea, and although it took a while Spit, and even Mamie and Bessie, became warmly hospitable to the fine young dog. They watched with rapt fascination as the workers tossed tennis balls for her to retrieve, and they welcomed her as she settled down and went to sleep only a short distance from wherever they might be.

Because of the carpenters' noise, I took an apartment a few minutes away to finish this book. It became something of a routine, in fact, my returning home every evening at about seven. Once he grew accustomed to this, Spit would be sitting there at the back of the driveway every day precisely at seven, his eyes glowingly caught in the headlights of my car, waiting for me. He knew I would be there. He would rush up to the car, and when I opened the door he would jump into my lap and welcome me back.

The carpenters took a strong liking to Spit. One of

them called him "a very fine cat, a very *smart* cat." Among them was a college graduate and fledgling young poet named Andy di Michele, who had four cats himself. Andy was inspired, he said, to write "a simple, ordinary poem about an extraordinary cat," but overcomplicated the first draft of his poem by having Spit spiritually blessed by the Egyptian cat-goddess Basket. When this did not work, he took Wallace Stevens's "Thirteen Ways of Looking at a Blackbird" as his "distant, ephemeral inspiration"—a day in the life of Spit McGee seen through Spit's eyes and his:

2 ways of looking at spit mcgee
1. One of spit's eyes is gold
     by which he keeps attuned
to the everyday shuffle of random events
and objects: 2 X 4s, a chocolate lab, the speeding
old ladies of brookdale drive or the sudden scream
     of a miter saw. This eye leads
spit across his own lawn
to stroll the margins of curb and grass

or pause to wash and define his daily empire.
2. with his blue eye Spit looks back at me
as he has each morning and walks under
ladders. coming or going, spit mcgee
          is a white cat, but i've never
noticed if he casts shadows.

Here is a translucent moment: a penetratingly cold winter's night, a staunch fire in the fireplace, and the cats and the Cat Woman comfortably ensconced in the den with me. A nut cake is baking in the oven, the fine wholesome aroma of it wafting through the house, and Spit, Mamie, and Bessie are curled together in a furry bundle in front of the fire. The whole world is closed out in this moment. This is my favorite family, and I would die for them. In all my American comings and goings it has seldom been much better than this, and as I look down at my cats I am gratified that they are safe, warm, and happy, and I think of all the poor, starved, mistreated animals out there in this bitter night everywhere, nameless and with no place to go—and the contentment and security of my own three cats assuage for me just a little this awareness of the vulnerability of God's abused and suffering creatures.

I suppose this has really been a little tale about time in its passing, as all stories must be—of life moving on, I think. The seasons change and Spit and I still go down to the creek, where the Choctaw Indians and the Anglo-Saxon farmers and the Yankee foot soldiers wandering over from the nearby fortifications of the pyrotechnic Sherman once roamed, to see what might be drifting down our way. The throaty croak of the indomitable bullfrog yet returns to us every springtime, providing a continuity to the seasons. How old must that bullfrog be now? The small things are the best part of life, although we seldom acknowledge this in their moment. I love the Saturday afternoons of highest autumn, the leaves of a dozen colors arcing down in our lawn, the air brisk and cool after the brutal, interminable summer, the distant sounds coming from very far away, and at the picnic table I listen to the college football games on the radio and watch Spit as he climbs the white oak tree, glad as he is to have an enthralling chill back in the air.

I have observed at close range four generations of one cat family over a time of nine years. These generations have been more immediate for me, more compressed, more accessible than human ones. I would exchange nothing for this opportunity. Against old mortality, life "is nothing but the continuity of its love," Eudora Welty wrote.

Unlike people and dogs, cats do not show their age very much. There must be a reason. Our neighbors across the way have an eighteen-year-old cat who could pass for four. Spit could be mistaken for three, and the calico Mamie and the orange-faced Bessie sometimes still look kittenish. We have a framed photograph on the wall that I study from time to time—of Rivers Applewhite, the first in the line, gazing at the camera's eye with her riveting, quizzical brown eyes.

As the reader may recall, after I had made my dismaying discovery nine long years ago that my fiancée was a Cat Woman, I desperately sought out people for advice. I still do this when I find someone particularly attuned to cats. Only last week I asked my now eleven-year-old friend Bailey Browne what she has learned from her cats. Since she alone is responsible for this book, for better or worse, ever having been written in the first place, I must share with you what she said. She needed little encouragement and promptly launched into an impromptu soliloquy.

"I've learned a lot about getting what I want from people by watching my cat Toots train my grandmother," she said. "Maw Maw moved in with us this summer, and at first all she did was complain about our cats. We've got three, you know—Spook, the momma; Bo, the girl baby; and Tootsie Roll, the boy baby. Then slowly I noticed a change. Maw Maw started talking *to* the cats instead of talking *about* them. Tootsie was becoming Maw Maw's favorite. Whenever she sat at her place at the table, there Tootsie lay at her feet. He'd sit and look up until she noticed him. Then he'd give her the smallest meow. If she didn't give him something he'd roll around on her feet. Then he'd nip on her ankle or claw on her thigh and a piece of chicken would be gone off her plate. Now she's so well trained Tootsie never has to resort to that.

"Kittens can always find the best spot in a room. A little while ago, not long ago, I was reading aloud from my history book and Toots responded to a name. It was a Kushite prince, Piankhi. I like kittens 'cause they're sweet, smart, cute, and they don't smell bad, even when they're wet. I think they're really little people in tiny kitty suits." Bailey went on: "Cats have taught me to look cute, act sweet, persist and get louder, and if all else fails, bring matters into your own teeth!"

Then, when she had finished, she asked, "What have *you* learned from cats?"

I thought for a while; my answer was a simple one. "I've learned to care for them on their own terms. And that I know they care for us a lot. And don't try to figure them out too much."

Sometimes I wake up and hear the Cat Woman in other parts of the house singing to our cats. One morning I heard her singing to Spit:

Night and day, you are the one. . . .

It was she who taught me that a dog man and incorrigible hater of cats could grow to honor them, and that the dog man himself could come to be whole again. Our very life together has been inseparable from the cats. So this story is about human love too.

Yet the main character in this book, as I intended all along, of course, is Spit McGee, and only he can end it.

Last Christmas David Rae gave me a framed portrait he had taken of Spit that, as with all fine photographs, captures much of his essence. His head is lifted in curiosity. There is rippling sunlight on his handsome countenance and pink nose and upright ears, and dark shadows on fallen leaves in the background, his blue and gold eyes gazing into the camera's eye with a look at once of inscrutability and bemusement and tenderness and mischief.

I will always remember his light tread on my worktable, how he sits there on my writing hand and looks into my eyes. I wonder to this day where he really came from—wonder too at the strange fate that, out of all of it, brought the two of us together in our mutual hour. If Old Skip was the ally of my boyhood, and Pete of my middle years, then what does it say about me that Spit is such the intimate comrade of my maturity? A dog is a companion, faithful, helpful, and generous; this companionship is consistent and predictable and you are so supremely fortunate that you can more or less take this for granted. But never once can I take Spit for granted, certainly not in that way. A person is in the company of cats, and cats insist they be treated as company. Spit demands his independence when it suits him, and his dependence in turn. He may be the quirkiest iconoclast I ever knew. Wondering why he does what he does is a source of endless reflection for me, for in the soul of him he is a wonderful mystery to me, and it could be that my friendship with him over these years somehow suggests that I myself have become a little more forebearing and, perhaps, complex.

On the death of his beloved fourteen-year-old cat named Cuddles, the author Kinky Friedman wrote, "People may surprise you with unexpected kindness. Dogs have a depth of loyalty that often we seem unworthy of. But the love of a cat is a blessing, a privilege in this world." Friedman received a sympathy note from his cat's veterinarian, which opened with a verse by Irving Townsend: "We who choose to surround ourselves with lives even more temporary than our own live within a fragile circle. . . ."

If I myself could choose a verse for Spit, it would be from Andrew Marvell: "Had we but world enough and time." Only yesterday I contemplated him perched in a branch of our oak tree. He was like a monarch of the jungle, lithe, regal, majestic, and serene, solitary in his mystic wits and strengths, assaying the scene below him— the sweeping greensward, the old house, Mamie, Bessie, and his human people. Yet moments later he descended from the tree and jumped onto the picnic table, where I was sitting, and hovered affectionately around me, not the imperious and lordly beast of his manor now, but like the little kitten of years ago who was always climbing my legs to rest in my lap.

This afternoon the two of us were down by the creek sitting together in our favorite spot. It was false spring again in January and the warming sunlight fell languidly upon us. As I stroked him on his back, once again he snuggled into my lap. "I love you, Spitty," I said. He extended his paw toward me. At the beginning of this story I confessed I had an odd writer's inkling that Spit might be my dog Skip reincarnated, sent back to earth by the Almighty to see if I was doing all right. But in that moment I affirmed in the deepest heart of me: Spit McGee is not Old Skip. Spit McGee is Spit McGee.

ABOUT THE AUTHOR

In addition to *My Dog Skip*, WILLIE MORRIS was also the author of *North Toward Home, New York Days,* and many other books. As the imaginative and creative editor of Harper's magazine, he was a major influence in changing our postwar literary and journalistic history. He died in 1999 in Jackson, Mississippi, where he lived with his wife, JoAnne, his friend Spit McGee, and his other cats, Mamie and Bessie.

Also by Wille Morris
and available in Beeler Large Print

My   Dog   Skip

In 1943 in a sleepy town on the Yazoo River, a boy fell in love with a puppy with a lively gait and an intelligent way of listening. The two grew up together having the most wonderful adventures— from run-ins with copperheads to a harrowing all-night vigil in a graveyard. **My Dog Skip** is a classic story of a boy and a dog and growing up in small-town America during the war years that belong on the same shelf as *The Adventures of Tom Sawyer* and Russell Baker's *Growing Up*. Poignant, funny, and unabashedly sweet-spirited, this is a book that will enchant readers of all ages for years to come.

Dear Reader:

I hope you enjoyed reading this Large Print book. If you are interested in reading other Beeler Large Print titles, ask your librarian or write to me at

> Thomas T. Beeler, *Publisher*
> Post Office Box 659
> Hampton Falls, New Hampshire 03844

You can also call me at 1-800-251-8726 and I will send you my latest catalogue.

Audrey Lesko and I choose the titles I publish in Large Print. Our aim is to provide good books by outstanding authors—books we both enjoyed reading and liked well enough to want to share. We warmly welcome any suggestions for new titles and authors.

Sincerely,

Tom Beeler